Jesus The Christ

Bible Studies, Volume 27

Leslie Rendell

Published by Leslie Rendell, 2024.

Table of Contents

Prelude

The story of our Lord Jesus Christ is a very complicated one. There are many aspects of his remarkable life that I will endeavour to cover in this book. But to cover his entire life would mean to rewrite the entire bible because that book is all about him. I will attempt to back up all of the claims I make in this book from the scriptures. I am in no way interested in the traditions and teachings of man. Only the word of God will give us the truth on all matters. What does John 17:17 say?

Joh 17:17 Sanctify them by the truth; your word is truth.

Why should we study the bible? Isn't it enough to go to church once a week and listen to the Pastor?

Most Pastors who belong to one of the modern-day churches have to follow what the church leaders tell them. They all have their own "statement of beliefs" to adhere to, and these doctrines vary from church to church in what they see as the truth. So since they cannot all be right, then some must be wrong. What if that refers to the church you are attending if indeed you attend any church at all? How can you know what God sees as the truth? Well, it is up to the individual to sort the wheat from the chaff. How do we do that? Only by seeking the truth that God has concealed in his book, the bible.

Consider the following passage of scripture in the book of Proverbs.

Pro 25:2 It is the glory of God to conceal things, but the glory of kings is to search things out.

This is what God expects from us. We are to look constantly into the holy scriptures and find the truth that he has concealed there for us to discover. Please notice that God has not concealed them from us to keep it all a secret. No, he wants us to look for the truth. This is further emphasized in the following verses from the book of Isaiah.

Isa 28:9 To whom will he teach knowledge, and to whom will he explain the message? Those who are weaned from the milk, those taken from the breast?

Isa 28:10 For it is precept upon precept, precept upon precept, line upon line, line upon line, here a little, there a little.

This backs up what we read in Proverbs 25:2: that we must search out a matter that God has concealed. This is a real treasure hunt. If we can seek the will of God in our lives, we are not rejecting him, but we are embracing him and his way of life. There is a glorious reward for those who are prepared to seek God with their whole hearts. Read the following verse and see what this reward is.

Rom 2:7 To those who by persistence in doing good seek glory, honor and immortality, he will give eternal life.

Therefore, we must spend time searching the scriptures. Looking for precept upon precept, line upon line, here a little, there a little. Looking for the things God has concealed. The Bible contains information on many topics, and the only way to find it is to spend time reading and searching the scriptures. There is no other substitute for Bible study. If we want the truth, then we must search for these pearls of wisdom. This is the advice we are given in the scriptures quoted above.

Who Is Jesus Christ

This book is all about God and His son Jesus Christ. Before we can delve into anything relating to God, we need to first of all decide if He even exists. Many atheists in the world simply cannot believe in the existence of an all-powerful creator God who brought all things into existence simply by the power of His word. Then there are millions of Christians who by faith believe in God.

So the first question we need to address is. Can we prove He exists?

This is a question without an exact answer. It is easy for someone to declare God does not exist, but it is impossible to prove it. Conversely, for those who do believe in God, there is much evidence that speaks of His existence.

The whole point of this is Christians who believe in God do so by faith because of two main reasons. First, there is the creation itself which speaks of a designer due to its complexity, wonders, and laws that keep the entire universe operating the way it does. Then we have the written word of God, His holy bible.

Regardless of what you believe, Jesus Christ is the most influential person in all of human history. Our modern calendars all start from the date of His birth, even though there is some discrepancy about the exact year of His birth.

I will not try to persuade you that Jesus exists, because this book is all about Him. Either you are a believer or you are not. There is no half-right or half-wrong when it comes to His existence. So I will assume you are seeking proof to reinforce your beliefs. Whether you are an atheist or a Christian.

If you believe in God, then the rest is easy. Just believe what He will reveal about Himself in his amazing book, "The Bible". And then look at His incredible handy work in the way nature has been created, the plants, animals, insects, birds, and the vast array of living things.

If on the other hand, you believe in evolution. Then there are many things you must prove, beyond any shadow of a doubt, that will back up what you believe. As more science is revealing a Creator caused our existence, then the theory of evolution is becoming more difficult to prove every day.

In my opinion, there is no way our human DNA could have evolved. It is just too complex to be an accident of evolution.

So now let us establish who Jesus Christ is. To do this, I will look into God's holy scriptures for an answer in the book of John. In the first eighteen verses of this book, we get a wonderful description of Jesus and just why we believe him to be the Messiah. Or the Son Of God.

Joh 1:1 In the beginning was the Word, and the Word was with God, and the Word was God.

Joh 1:2 The same was in the beginning with God.

Joh 1:3 All things were made through him. Without him was not anything made that has been made.

Joh 1:4 In him was life, and the life was the light of men.

Joh 1:5 The light shines in the darkness, and the darkness hasn't overcome it.

Joh 1:6 There came a man, sent from God, whose name was John.

Joh 1:7 The same came as a witness, that he might testify about the light, that all might believe through him.

Joh 1:8 He was not the light, but was sent that he might testify about the light.

Joh 1:9 The true light that enlightens everyone was coming into the world.

Joh 1:10 He was in the world, and the world was made through him, and the world didn't recognize him.

Joh 1:11 He came to his own, and those who were his own didn't receive him.

Joh 1:12 But as many as received him, to them he gave the right to become God's children, to those who believe in his name:

Joh 1:13 who were born not of blood, nor of the will of the flesh, nor of the will of man, but of God.

Joh 1:14 The Word became flesh, and lived among us. We saw his glory, such glory as of the one and only Son of the Father, full of grace and truth.

Joh 1:15 John testified about him. He cried out, saying, "This was he of whom I said, 'He who comes after me has surpassed me, for he was before me.'"

Joh 1:16 From his fullness we all received grace upon grace.

Joh 1:17 For the law was given through Moses. Grace and truth were realized through Jesus Christ.

Joh 1:18 No one has seen God at any time. The one and only Son, who is in the bosom of the Father, he has declared him.

What does this section of scripture tell us? From verse one, we see "The Word" was with God and he was God. Then we learn "The Word" was responsible for creating all things. There is nothing in all the vast universe that he did not bring into existence. This "Word" then became flesh and dwelt among us and made God The Father known to everyone who will believe.

Whoever "The Word" may be, he is a powerful person and we can deduce from the scriptures above that "The Word" is, in fact Jesus Christ. This thought is reinforced in Joh 1:29.

Joh 1:29 The next day, he saw Jesus coming to him, and said, "Behold, the Lamb of God, who takes away the sin of the world!

Now John, known as "John the Baptist," sees Jesus coming to be baptised by him in the river. He declares Jesus to be the Lamb of God who takes away the sins of the world.

This same Jesus Christ is the one who was crucified, buried, and resurrected as I will explain in the rest of this book. By proving Jesus was, in reality, resurrected from the dead, we are also proving the divinity of Jesus Christ. We also prove the validity of those first eighteen verses of the book of John.

One thing I would like to clarify here is the name of our Lord. Jesus is his name in English, but his Hebrew name is Yeshua. The word Christ is not a name but a title that means. The anointed one, or the Messiah. So to say Jesus Christ is to say, Jesus the Messiah. The Son of God.

Jesus Christ In Prophecy

Many people in the world do not believe in our Lord Jesus Christ and therefore do not believe that he ever rose from the dead. How can we prove firstly that he even existed? Well, even the Jewish Rabbis from the time of Jesus did not like him or his followers. They hated him so much that they had him crucified on a Roman cross.

A terrible form of execution that caused as much pain and suffering as possible. They accused him of being a magician and of leading people away from their religion. But the one thing that they never did was to claim that he never existed. There is enough proof in history books that will prove that Jesus Christ was an actual person.

The Muslims, who hate both Jews and Christians also believe that Jesus was a real person. They claim he was a prophet, but do not acknowledge that he is God. There is a lot of other information about Jesus apart from the bible that back up the fact that Jesus did exist, and from the bible we can also believe he still exists.

Then there are the many prophecies in the Old Testament of the Bible that point directly to Jesus. Some are a little obscure, but some also clearly point to the man Jesus Christ. Look at what the Prophet Isaiah wrote about this amazing man about seven hundred years before Jesus was born. His description of Jesus in chapter fifty-three is remarkable and is a perfect description of the life and death of Jesus. He told of a man who would die for the sins of the world. Read Isaiah fifty-three and see the amazing resemblance to the life of Jesus Christ as has been recorded for us in the bible.

Isa 53:1 Who has believed our message? To whom has the arm of Yahweh been revealed?

Isa 53:2 For he grew up before him as a tender plant, and as a root out of dry ground. He has no good looks or majesty. When we see him, there is no beauty that we should desire him.

Isa 53:3 He was despised, and rejected by men; a man of suffering, and acquainted with disease. He was despised as one from whom men hide their face; and we didn't respect him.

Isa 53:4 Surely he has borne our sickness, and carried our suffering; yet we considered him plagued, struck by God, and afflicted.

Isa 53:5 But he was pierced for our transgressions. He was crushed for our iniquities. The punishment that brought our peace was on him; and by his wounds we are healed.

Isa 53:6 All we like sheep have gone astray. Everyone has turned to his own way; and Yahweh has laid on him the iniquity of us all.

Isa 53:7 He was oppressed, yet when he was afflicted he didn't open his mouth. As a lamb that is led to the slaughter, and as a sheep that before its shearers is silent, so he didn't open his mouth.

Isa 53:8 He was taken away by oppression and judgement; and as for his generation, who considered that he was

cut off out of the land of the living and stricken for the disobedience of my people?

Isa 53:9 They made his grave with the wicked, and with a rich man in his death; although he had done no violence,

nor was any deceit in his mouth.

Isa 53:10 Yet it pleased Yahweh to bruise him. He has caused him to suffer. When you make his soul an offering for sin, he will see his offspring. He will prolong his days, and Yahweh's pleasure will prosper in his hand.

Isa 53:11 After the suffering of his soul, he will see the light and be satisfied. My righteous servant will justify many by the knowledge of himself; and he will bear their iniquities.

Isa 53:12 Therefore I will give him a portion with the great, and he will divide the plunder with the strong; because he poured out his soul to death, and was counted with the transgressors; yet he bore the sins of many, and made intercession for the transgressors.

When you realize that this passage of scripture was written about seven hundred years before Jesus came on the scene, you see a very accurate portrayal of the life and death of our Lord. There are many other prophecies recorded for us in the Bible, but I think this one gives us the most vivid picture of Jesus Christ.

I believe that when you combine historical facts with prophecies, there can be very little doubt about whether Jesus Christ was a real person. To claim Jesus never existed is to ignore the evidence in both the history books and the revelations found about him in the bible.

Once you come to believe Jesus was, and still is real today, you are well on the road to accepting him as your Lord and God. Jesus made some amazing claims in the approximately three and a half years he was spreading the gospel. His greatest claim was that he was the Messiah, the Son of God. He even predicted he would be arrested, betrayed, spit upon, scourged, and then killed. The similarities between his life and the prophecy of Isaiah are unmistakable. Jesus also told the leaders of the synagogue and his disciples that he would be raised to life after three days. This incredible prediction has been recorded for us in the book of Mark, chapter ten and verses thirty-two through to thirty-four.

Mar 10:32 They were on the way, going up to Jerusalem; and Jesus was going in front of them, and they were amazed; and those who followed were afraid. He again took the twelve, and began to tell them the things that were going to happen to him.

Mar 10:33 "Behold, we are going up to Jerusalem. The Son of Man will be delivered to the chief priests and the scribes. They will condemn him to death, and will deliver him to the Gentiles."

*Mar 10:34 They will mock him, spit on him, scourge him, and kill him.
On the third day he will rise again.*

It would be a very brave man indeed to make such a claim if he was not sure
of his facts. Until this time, no one had ever come back from the dead.

The Jewish Pharisees and Sadducees knew their Old Testament scriptures
very well. Many of them could recite the scriptures by heart. Some prophecies
about the coming of their Messiah were very clear, so at about the time Jesus
came on the scene, they were already expecting him to come.

They read and understood from the prophecies that their Messiah was due
to arrive on the earth. The problem for them is that they did not see him
coming as a suffering servant who was going to die for them to save everyone
from their sins. No, what they were expecting was a conquering King who
would overpower the Romans. They missed the reason for his coming, so
they refused to acknowledge that Jesus could be the Messiah. Their dream of
freedom from the Romans hung on the arrival of their Messiah.

These Jewish leaders demanded a sign from Jesus to prove he was the
Messiah they were looking for. Read Mat 16:1-4 and see these Pharisees and the
Sadducees challenging Jesus to prove he was who he claimed to be and Christ's
reply to them.

*Mat 12:38 Then certain of the scribes and Pharisees answered,
"Teacher, we want to see a sign from you."*

*Mat 12:39 But he answered them, "An evil and adulterous generation
seeks after a sign, but no sign will be given*

to it but the sign of Jonah the prophet.

*Mat 12:40 For as Jonah was three days and three nights in the belly of
the whale, so will the Son of Man be three days and three nights in the
heart of the earth.*

Jesus' answer to these Pharisees, and the Sadducees, was a prophecy about
his soon-coming death and resurrection. Here Jesus tells them he would be
three days and three nights in the tomb, the exact time Jonah was in the whale's

belly. It is important to note one thing from this section of scripture. Jesus told them the "ONLY SIGN" he would give them was the sign of Jonah that we read above in verse forty.

Everything that Jesus taught, and the claim that he was the Messiah, all hinged on him fulfilling exactly the sign of Jonah. He was to be exactly three days and three nights in the tomb. If he was more or less than this period in the tomb, then he must be a fraud and an impostor. This was going to be the ultimate test of the authenticity of Jesus Christ. If you can prove that he got it wrong and that he was not in the tomb for this exact amount of time, then he is a fraud. But then if we can prove that he was in the tomb for exactly three days and three nights, fulfilling precisely the "sign of Jonah", we have found our Messiah!

The resurrection from the dead of our Lord and Saviour Jesus Christ is one of the most important of all Christian beliefs. All Christians today must believe that Jesus was resurrected from the dead, otherwise, they have nothing to base their faith in him upon. It is only by his defeating the last enemy, and that is death, that we can have any genuine hope of a future with him.

There is only one way to prove if Jesus is who he claims to be, and that is to search the scriptures for the answer and accept what we learn from these sacred words as the truth. Did he fulfill this sign he gave to the Jewish leaders of his day, or did he fail this test or sign?

One thing that is for certain, and I hope anyone, regardless of what they believe, will agree upon. If Jesus rose from the dead as he claimed he would. Then how can he possibly not be the Son Of God, and if he is the Son of God, then what is stopping people from accepting him into their lives?

If he did not rise from the dead, then he is a fake and an impostor and therefore someone we should not follow or worship. Since there is so much depending on the truthful answer to this question, we need to be thorough and believe only what God has revealed to us.

The Apostle Paul, in his letter to the Corinthians, made the importance of answering this question correctly when he said the following in 1Co 15:19.

> *1Co 15:19 If we have only hoped in Christ in this life, we are of all men most pitiable.*

The Apostle Paul put it very well here. If Jesus is a fake, then the disciples who followed Jesus, and right down to the millions of Christians who follow him today, have been fed a massive lie. We have no future in God's Kingdom and therefore no hope in all the world. That is why it is vital to study carefully this topic and come to the right conclusion.

One thing I still find amazing is the disciples who were with Jesus for just over three years did not fully understand what Jesus had told them about his death, and the amazing event that was going to follow in three days. By this time, they had seen many miracles, and they certainly understood Jesus was "The Christ". We read this in Luke chapter nine and verses eighteen through twenty.

> *Luk 9:18 As he was praying alone, the disciples were with him, and he asked them, "Who do the multitudes say that I am?"*

> *Luk 9:19 They answered, "John the Baptizer," but others say, 'Elijah,' and others, that one of the old prophets is risen again."*

> *Luk 9:20 He said to them, "But who do you say that I am?" Peter answered, "The Christ of God."*

So the disciples understood who Jesus was, and we see in the next two verses where Jesus told them he must suffer many things and be rejected by the elders. But even though the disciples heard these words, they could not truly believe them. They also, like the Jewish leaders, failed to see why Jesus had come down from heaven.

> *Luk 9:21 But he warned them, and commanded them to tell this to no one,*

> *Luk 9:22 saying, "The Son of Man must suffer many things, and be rejected by the elders, chief priests, and scribes, and be killed, and the third day be raised up."*

Again, in these verses, we see Jesus predicting his death and that he was going to be raised to life on the third day. Remember, this was the only sign we have that Jesus Christ is our Messiah.

Luke recorded again in Luk 18:31-34 what Jesus told his disciples about his death and resurrection. Then recognise from the last verse that his disciples did not understand what he was saying, the truth was hidden from them.

Luk 18:31 He took the twelve aside, and said to them, "Behold, we are going up to Jerusalem, and all the things that are written through the prophets concerning the Son of Man will be completed.

Luk 18:32 For he will be delivered up to the Gentiles, will be mocked, treated shamefully, and spit on.

Luk 18:33 They will scourge and kill him. On the third day, he will rise again."

Luk 18:34 They understood none of these things. This saying was hidden from them, and they didn't understand the things that were said.

Before I get into the proof of Jesus being in the tomb for exactly three days and three nights, I would like to see more proof that he is the "Son of God".

So, what is the evidence that we can see in these Ancient Words that can help us believe Jesus Christ is The Son Of God and has indeed risen from the dead?

More Prophecies referring to Jesus

Some biblical scholars have calculated there are somewhere around 300 prophecies about Jesus Christ in the Old Testament. Some of these prophecies are very specific and are meant to point to Jesus Christ.

It has been calculated that for Jesus to fulfil just 8 of these prophecies is 1 in 10 to the power of 17. That is 10 followed by 17 zeros. What would the answer be if they calculated for all 300 prophecies? The number would be astronomical.

Let us now look at just a few of these prophecies in the Old Testament, and then see where they were fulfilled in the New Testament.

<u>The Virgin Birth of Jesus Christ</u>
Prophecy:

Isa 7:14 Therefore the Lord himself will give you a sign: The virgin will conceive and give birth to a son, and will call him Immanuel.

Fulfillment:

Luk 1:35 The angel answered, "The Holy Spirit will come on you, and the power of the Most High will overshadow you. So the holy one to be born will be called the Son of God.

<u>Jesus would come out of Egypt:</u>
Prophecy:

Hos 11:1 "When Israel was a child, I loved him, and out of Egypt I called my son.

Fulfillment:

Mat 2:14 So he got up, took the child and his mother during the night and left for Egypt,

Mat 2:15 where he stayed until the death of Herod. And so was fulfilled what the Lord had said through the prophet: "Out of Egypt I called my son."

Jesus was to be born in Bethlehem:
Prophecy:

Mic 5:2 "But you, Bethlehem Ephrathah, though you are small among the clans of Judah, out of you will come for me one who will be ruler over Israel, whose origins are from of old, from ancient times."

Fulfillment:

Mat 2:4 When he had called together all the people's chief priests and teachers of the law, he asked them where the Messiah was to be born.

Mat 2:5 "In Bethlehem in Judea," they replied, "for this is what the prophet has written:

Mat 2:6 "'But you, Bethlehem, in the land of Judah, are by no means least among the rulers of Judah; for out of you will come a ruler who will shepherd my people Israel.'"

Jesus would use parables to teach:
Prophecy:

Psa 78:1 A maskil of Asaph. My people, hear my teaching; listen to the words of my mouth.

Psa 78:2 I will open my mouth with a parable; I will utter hidden things, things from of old—

Psa 78:3 things we have heard and known, things our ancestors have told us.

Fulfillment:

Mat 13:34 Jesus spoke all these things to the crowd in parables; he did not say anything to them without using a parable.

Mat 13:35 So was fulfilled what was spoken through the prophet: "I will open my mouth in parables, I will utter things hidden since the creation of the world."

<u>People would not understand the parables:</u>
Prophecy:

Isa 6:9 He said, "Go and tell this people: '"Be ever hearing, but never understanding; be ever seeing, but never perceiving.'

Isa 6:10 Make the heart of this people calloused; make their ears dull and close their eyes. Otherwise they might see with their eyes, hear with their ears, understand with their hearts, and turn and be healed."

Fulfillment:

Mat 13:13 This is why I speak to them in parables: "Though seeing, they do not see; though hearing, they do not hear or understand.

Mat 13:14 In them is fulfilled the prophecy of Isaiah: '"You will be ever hearing but never understanding; you will be ever seeing but never perceiving.

Mat 13:15 For this people's heart has become calloused; they hardly hear with their ears, and they have closed their eyes. Otherwise they might see with their eyes, hear with their ears, understand with their hearts and turn, and I would heal them.'

<u>Jesus was to be the perfect sacrifice:</u>
Prophecy:

Psa 40:6 Sacrifice and offering you did not desire— but my ears you have opened— burnt offerings and sin offerings you did not require.

Psa 40:7 Then I said, "Here I am, I have come— it is written about me in the scroll.

Psa 40:8 I desire to do your will, my God; your law is within my heart."

Fulfillment:

Heb 10:5 Therefore, when Christ came into the world, he said: "Sacrifice and offering you did not desire, but a body you prepared for me;

Heb 10:6 with burnt offerings and sin offerings you were not pleased.

Heb 10:7 Then I said, 'Here I am—it is written about me in the scroll— I have come to do your will, my God.'"

Heb 10:8 First he said, "Sacrifices and offerings, burnt offerings and sin offerings you did not desire, nor were you pleased with them"—though they were offered in accordance with the law.

Heb 10:9 Then he said, "Here I am, I have come to do your will." He sets aside the first to establish the second.

Heb 10:10 And by that will, we have been made holy through the sacrifice of the body of Jesus Christ once for all.

This prophecy is truly amazing. King David wrote this psalm and he tells us *"Sacrifice and offering you did not desire."* Then he says *"I desire to do your will, my God; your law is within my heart."*

The fulfilment of this prophecy in Heb 10:9 Is where we learn the Old Testament has been replaced with the New Testament. Then in the next verse we are given the guarantee the sacrifice of Jesus on the cross has made all those who believe in him holy.

<u>The Nations would be blessed through Abraham:</u>

Prophecy:

Gen 12:1 The LORD had said to Abram, "Go from your country, your people and your father's household to the land I will show you.

Gen 12:2 "I will make you into a great nation, and I will bless you; I will make your name great, and you will be a blessing.

Gen 12:3 I will bless those who bless you, and whoever curses you I will curse; and all peoples on earth will be blessed through you."

Fulfillment:

Act 3:25 And you are heirs of the prophets and of the covenant God made with your fathers. He said to Abraham, 'Through your offspring all peoples on earth will be blessed.'

Act 3:26 When God raised up his servant, he sent him first to you to bless you by turning each of you from your wicked ways."

These 7 examples of prophecies that point to Jesus Christ were recorded so we can see Jesus Christ is who he claims to be.

Furthermore, this is a perfect example of what I wrote in the "Prelude" to this book that we must search the scriptures to find truths God has concealed for us to seek out.

Pro 25:2 It is the glory of God to conceal things, but the glory of kings is to search things out.

Miracles of Jesus

Jesus performed many miracles during his time on the earth. He healed the sick, gave sight to the blind, cured cripples, and even cleansed people from leprosy. Still, most of his miracles were never recorded in the books of the Bible, as we can see from Joh 20:30.

Joh 20:30 Jesus performed many other signs in the presence of his disciples, which are not recorded in this book.

Jesus performed one powerful miracle that had a profound effect on his disciples. This miracle that involved the disciples was when they were crossing the lake and a fierce storm arose and threatened to swamp their boat. We must remember that these men were all experienced fishermen and had spent their lives on the lake and would have encountered many storms. This storm was one of the worst that they had ever encountered, and we can know this from their call for Jesus to rescue them. We can read this in Matthew 8:23-27.

Mat 8:23 When he got into a boat, his disciples followed him.

Mat 8:24 Behold, a violent storm came up on the sea, so much that the boat was covered with the waves, but he was asleep.

Mat 8:25 They came to him, and woke him up, saying, "Save us, Lord! We are dying!"

Mat 8:26 He said to them, "Why are you fearful, O you of little faith?" Then he got up, rebuked the wind and the sea, and there was a great calm.

Mat 8:27 The men marvelled, saying, "What kind of man is this, that even the wind and the sea obey him?"

In verse twenty-seven, they ask, "What kind of man is this?". Here, they witnessed how Jesus even had control of the elements and did what no man had ever done before. He stopped the furious storm and caused a complete calmness over the lake. This miracle alone would have had them believing that Jesus had powers that only belonged to God. But I doubt they were fully convinced who was with them in the boat. They asked, "What kind of man is this".

Another miracle they witnessed was recorded for us in Matthew 14:22-33. This time, the disciples had left Jesus on the shore and were crossing the lake when another storm rose and threatened to swamp their boat. Suddenly Jesus appeared to them walking up to the boat on the water and again calmed the wind. This time the Disciples make the correct connection about just who Jesus is, when they say, "Truly, you are the Son of God."

There are many other miracles recorded in the Bible that the disciples of Jesus saw and marveled at. Such as feeding the four thousand, healing the lepers, and curing the paralysed man who was lowered through the roof. These are just a few of the recorded miracles we know of, but there were other miracles that he performed and that were witnessed by the disciples but never recorded.

The disciples must have witnessed hundreds of miracles ranging from small and almost insignificant to some of his biggest miracles. Such as feeding the 5 thousand and calming the sea. Those three and a half years must have been mind-blowing for the disciples. Seeing the power Jesus possessed should have left no doubt in their minds if Jesus was the Son of God. But as we will see later in this book, it was not until after Jesus was resurrected from the dead that they were all fully convinced he was their Messiah.

The disciples of Jesus were with him for about three and a half years. During this time, they would have witnessed many miracles, and as we saw above, they realised Jesus was someone unique. But they did not fully understand he was God until after he rose from the dead. It was only his resurrection that fully convinced his disciples he was God. Therefore, it is vital for us today to come to the same conclusion as they came to. Jesus Christ is God.

The Disciples of Jesus Christ

The term disciple comes from the Greek word "Mathetes". This refers to a student of a philosopher. The disciples were also know as Apostles in the New Testament.

There is a slight difference in the meanings of these words. But they are both good words to describe these twelve men who followed Jesus.

A Disciple is a student who is learning from their leader. They lived with him most of the time and tried to live according to what they were learning from him. They heard the words of Jesus, but they would have derived more benefit from learning about his character, from seeing the miracles he performed and about who he is portrayed himself to be.

Now the term Apostle. This means, one who is sent. And this also perfectly describes who these twelve men were. They were with Jesus to learn, and then Jesus sent them out into the world to proclaim the gospel to the entire world.

So both these titles fit well with these twelve men who followed Jesus and were then sent to teach others about the coming "Kingdom Of God".

The disciples of Jesus were with him for about 3 1/2 years. It is very interesting to see how they changed in that time. As you read the rest of this book, you will see the change in their attitudes from being afraid to being dynamic preachers of "The Gospel".

What is The Gospel? all this word means is the good news, and if you are willing to believe the bible, then you will see just how good the news is for your future.

The Disciples Were Afraid

The disciples, who would have been the most convinced that Jesus was the anointed One, still did not understand what Jesus had so clearly told them. Their faith and trust in him were not strong, and they were afraid for their safety. We can see how they reacted when Jesus was arrested. We can read about this in Matthew 26:54-56 when Jesus was about to be arrested in the garden of Gethsemane.

Mat 26:54 How then would the Scriptures be fulfilled that it must be so?"

Mat 26:55 In that hour Jesus said to the multitudes, "Have you come out as against a robber with swords and clubs to seize me? I sat daily in the temple teaching, and you didn't arrest me."

Mat 26:56 But all this has happened, that the Scriptures of the prophets might be fulfilled. "Then all the disciples left him, and fled".

Yes, these disciples (who all believed that Jesus was the Son Of God) fled for their safety even though they were witnesses to his miracles and believed him to be The Son of God. Even Peter was afraid of the Jews and did not want to be recognized as one of his disciples. But he was still curious enough to follow at a distance to see what was going to happen to Jesus. We can read of this in Luke, chapter twenty-two, and verses fifty-four to sixty-two.

Luk 22:54 They seized him, and led him away, and brought him into the high priest's house. But Peter followed from a distance.

Luk 22:55 When they had kindled a fire in the middle of the courtyard, and had sat down together, Peter sat among them.

Luk 22:56 A certain servant girl saw him as he sat in the light, and looking intently at him, said, "This man also was with him."

Luk 22:57 He denied Jesus, saying, "Woman, I don't know him."

Luk 22:58 After a little while someone else saw him, and said, "You also are one of them!" But Peter answered, "Man, I am not!"

Luk 22:59 After about one hour passed, another confidently affirmed, saying, "Truly this man also was with him, for he is a Galilean!"

Luk 22:60 But Peter said, "Man, I don't know what you are talking about!" Immediately, while he was still speaking, a rooster crowed.

Luk 22:61 The Lord turned, and looked at Peter. Then Peter remembered the Lord's word, how he said to him, "Before the rooster crows you will deny me three times."

Luk 22:62 He went out, and wept bitterly.

Peter had earlier in verse thirty-three said, "Lord, I am ready to go with you to prison and to death". Yet here he was denying three times he even knew Jesus. He had earlier declared that Jesus "was the Messiah". But in the final crunch, Peter was anxious for his welfare, so he took the simple way out and denied that he knew Jesus. The rest of the disciples went into hiding. These men were sure he was the Son of God, but they were still more concerned with their welfare and safety. Their faith was weak and more proof was needed that he was who he claimed to be.

The same thing can be said about us today. Our faith in Jesus is not strong when we first believe. It is only after more proof has been discovered can we have a strong enough faith in Jesus to dedicate our lives to him. Our faith, trust, belief, and love for him will not happen in an instant. No, it will only come from regular and consistent bible study. That is the aim of this book, to strengthen our faith and love for our Lord.

Not Expecting The Resurrection

We know the disciples were not expecting Jesus to be resurrected from the dead, because if they understood this, then they would have been waiting at the tomb after three days, ready to celebrate. Maybe with six earthen jars filled with water and hoping for a repeat of his first miracle.

But instead of waiting and looking for his resurrection, the disciples were afraid of what the leaders of the Synagogue may do to them, so they were hiding from them. Two of the disciples were on the road to Emmaus, which is a short distance from Jerusalem. They were trying to understand what had happened on Calvary.

The man they thought was their Messiah had been executed by the Romans, so their dreams of him setting up his kingdom on the earth were shattered. They were not expecting Jesus to be raised from the dead, so they were on their way home. These two men were joined on their walk by a man whom they did not recognize and who taught them everything that was to happen to their Messiah, as was written in their scriptures, the Old Testament. Suddenly, they realized who this man was when Jesus disclosed himself to them as they were breaking bread.

The women who had followed Jesus from the first day were not expecting Jesus to be resurrected either. They must have been demoralized by the events that had taken place on the day Jesus was crucified. We read in the epistles that they were preparing the spices and perfumes that were needed to prepare his body for burial. Even though Jesus had spoken of his resurrection, nobody understood just what this meant. The women went to the tomb to anoint the body of Jesus. They did not expect to find that the tomb was empty.

The disciples were all afraid of the Jews. After three and a half years of following Jesus, they now had the humiliating feeling that they were the laughingstock of all Jerusalem and were too embarrassed to go out, so they hid in the upper rooms. They also feared what the leaders of the Synagogue would do to them. They had just seen Jesus tortured and crucified, so they may have been fearing the same fate if they were caught. I think we can understand the predicament the disciples now found themselves in.

There was no one at the tomb after the third day because no one understood what Jesus had said regarding his death and resurrection.

For me, the one event in the entire Bible that convinces me that Jesus is the real deal has to be the story of his resurrection, and how this event changes the lives of his disciples. Their entire worlds were turned upside down and their behavior changed. The Disciples went from hiding from everyone to being powerful and unafraid witnesses for their Lord. They had seen many miracles that Jesus performed during their time with him; After they had witnessed blind men regaining their sight, paralyzed men being able to walk again, Lazarus coming back from the dead must have been a convincing miracle that should have left them in no doubt just who was there with them. But it was only after they saw Jesus rise from the dead that their trust and faith in him became unshakable.

After Jesus was crucified, and before he was raised from the dead, this period must have been the worst time in the lives of the Disciples. They had found their Messiah, seen his miracles, and then witnessed the unthinkable as the man they believed was the Son of God was murdered on the cross. Can we imagine how we would have felt if we were in their shoes?

Now we have the advantage of hindsight and know how the story ends, but the disciples did not have this advantage, they would have been left shattered.

What was going through the minds of the Disciples? They would have been devastated, confused, sad, and with about a thousand emotions running through their minds. These men had lost their Lord and had no one to turn to and explain to them just what had happened and just what the future may hold for them now that Jesus was dead. When Jesus was with them, they were no doubt considering their places in the Kingdom of God. Now, suddenly, these dreams were taken away from them.

Jesus Appears To The Disciples

After Jesus rose from the dead, he appeared to his disciples when they were in an upper room. This is the first time that Jesus appeared to the disciples after his crucifixion. We see here that the disciples had locked the door for fear of the Jewish leaders, so they spent the last three days hiding and fearing the Synagogue leaders.

Can we imagine how the disciples felt now? Confused, happy, excited, elated, and ecstatic, there would have been another thousand emotions running through their minds. But this time they would have differed totally from those they experienced just three short days ago.

Now they had their Messiah back from the dead, and if they had any doubts about whether he was the Son of God, these doubts would now have been dispelled from their minds.

This was the ultimate proof they needed, and after this, these men were so convinced of what they knew, they were prepared to suffer many things for the Lord, and indeed they did. Their lives would now never be the same.

Not a lot of information has survived about the fate of these men, but here is what's available from various sources, including the New Testament itself, apocryphal texts, early Christian historians, legends, and lore.

Andrew was crucified.

Bartholomew was crucified.

James, the son of Alphaeus, was crucified.

James, the son of Zebedee, was killed by the sword.

John died at a good old age and of natural causes, the only one to do so.

Matthew was crucified.

Peter was crucified upside down.

Philip was crucified.

Simon was crucified.

Thaddeus was killed by arrows.

Thomas died of a spear thrust.

Some of these reports are indeed accurate and some may be a little more uncertain, but it is well believed that all the men (except for John) met very premature and violent deaths. All but John died at a relatively young age and their deaths were violent and no doubt painful.

The difference between before the resurrection, to after the resurrection is remarkable. These men went from hiding to being the founders of the new church. When they were filled with the Holy Spirit, there was no stopping them. Please read Acts chapter four and verses twenty-nine to thirty-one.

Act 4:29 Now, Lord, look at their threats, and grant to your servants to speak your word with all boldness,

Act 4:30 while you stretch out your hand to heal; and that signs and wonders may be done through the name of

your holy Servant Jesus.

Act 4:31 When they had prayed, the place was shaken where they were gathered together. They were all filled with the Holy Spirit, and they spoke the word of God with boldness.

The Apostles were now speaking with authority and power and there was no way the Jewish leaders, or the Romans, were going to deter them from the task that Jesus had set before them. Now they had their futures laid out before them, and that was all they needed to withstand all threats and punishments that were handed out to them. So, ten of the original twelve were martyred because of their love and trust in Jesus. (Judas, who betrayed Jesus, committed suicide). John lived to a good old age and died of natural causes. After the resurrection, the Apostles became bold in their preaching. This was when they stopped being afraid and put their total trust in their Lord.

Jesus Appears To Others

The Apostles were not the only ones to see the risen Christ, as we can read in 1Co 15:5-8.

1Co 15:5 and that he appeared to Cephas, then to the twelve.

1Co 15:6 Then he appeared to over five hundred brothers at once, most of whom remain until now, but some have also fallen asleep.

1Co 15:7 Then he appeared to James, then to all the apostles,

1Co 15:8 and last of all, as to the child born at the wrong time, he appeared to me also.

The five hundred that he appeared to in verse six would have been the founding members of the early church, and because of persecution, they spread around the world, taking the knowledge of Jesus with them to all parts of the world.

We have the witness of many people that Jesus was indeed resurrected from the dead, and because of this incredible event that has been recorded for us, we can all rest easy knowing that this event is a fact of history, and that we can rely upon all the other promises that we have been given about our futures in the Kingdom of God.

The reason that the disciples all believed that Jesus was resurrected is because they all saw it with their own eyes, as was recorded in 1Jn 1:1-3.

1Jn 1:1 That which was from the beginning, that which we have heard, that which we have seen with our eyes, that which we saw, and our hands touched, concerning the Word of life

1Jn 1:2 (and the life was revealed, and we have seen, and testify, and declare to you the life, the eternal life, which was with the Father, and was revealed to us); our fellowship is with the Father, and with his Son, Jesus Christ.

We must believe in the risen Jesus Christ. Then we can have fellowship with God the Father and with Jesus Christ Himself.

Our Friend Doubting Thomas

The changes that came over the disciples were incredible. But the most amazing of all, and the one that should help us all in our journey of faith, is the experience of our good friend that we know as, "doubting Thomas". Consider his attitude after the crucifixion of Jesus and before he saw Him resurrected from the dead. In John 20:19-25, we see Thomas refusing to believe what his fellow disciples were trying to tell him about Jesus being resurrected from the dead.

Read this account in Joh 20:19-25.

Joh 20:19 On the evening of that first day of the week, when the disciples were together, with the doors locked for fear of the Jewish leaders, Jesus came and stood among them and said, "Peace be with you!"

Joh 20:20 After he said this, he showed them his hands and side. The disciples were overjoyed when they saw the Lord.

Joh 20:21 Again Jesus said, "Peace be with you! As the Father has sent me, I am sending you."

Joh 20:22 And with that he breathed on them and said, "Receive the Holy Spirit.

Joh 20:23 If you forgive anyone's sins, their sins are forgiven; if you do not forgive them, they are not forgiven."

Joh 20:24 Now Thomas (also known as Didymus), one of the Twelve, was not with the disciples when Jesus came.

Joh 20:25 So the other disciples told him, "We have seen the Lord!" But he said to them, "Unless I see the nail marks in his hands and put my finger where the nails were, and put my hand into his side, I will not believe."

We can see from verse 24 that Thomas was not present when Jesus first presented himself to the other disciples. We must remember Thomas had spent the last three years intimately acquainted with Jesus. Witnessing all his miracles and even hearing his prophecies about his coming death and resurrection, as has been recorded for us in Matthew chapter 16 and verse 21. That, and the testimony from the other ten disciples about Jesus' resurrection, should have been enough to convince him Jesus was indeed resurrected from the dead. But because he had not seen Jesus, he could not believe the impossible. That someone could come back from the grave. So he continued to not believe.

I can just imagine the other disciples trying to convince Thomas that the Lord had indeed risen from the dead. They would have tried every form of persuasion to get Thomas to believe them, but we can see in verse 25 what Thomas thought. He was not about to take anyone's word for it. He had to see the evidence for himself. "Unless I see in his hands the print of the nails, put my finger into the print of the nails, and put my hand into his side, I will not believe."

He had already seen Jesus Crucified and buried, so he needed actual proof before he would believe that Jesus was resurrected. And the longer Jesus stayed away, the more adamant, and the more determined Thomas would have been in his thoughts, and the more he would have said, "I will not believe". If Jesus had never shown Himself to Thomas, then Thomas would have never believed that Jesus had indeed risen from the dead.

We read in the next verse in John chapter 20: 26, that it was a week later before Jesus showed Himself to his disciples again. I think those 7 days between his first and second appearances to his disciples tell a very interesting and powerful story. One that is very easy to just read over and not consider the full and true meaning of this period.

Can you imagine these 7 days? If the Disciples slept for 8 hours a day, then they were awake for about one hundred and twelve hours, and just what do you think they were talking about? They may have still been arguing about who was to be the greatest in the Kingdom, who was to sit at his right hand and who at his left, and no doubt wondering how Jesus was now going to kick the Romans out of Jerusalem. But I think their major topic of conversation for those days would have been about their resurrected Lord, and how things might now change.

But what about Thomas for those one hundred and twelve hours? He must have been wondering what was wrong with the last bottle of wine the others had drunk to believe such a thing. People do not come back from the dead. We know from the next three verses that he kept this attitude for the full seven days.

Joh 20:26 A week later his disciples were in the house again, and Thomas was with them. Though the doors were locked, Jesus came and stood among them and said, "Peace be with you!"

Joh 20:27 Then he said to Thomas, "Put your finger here; see my hands. Reach out your hand and put it into my side. Stop doubting and believe."

Joh 20:28 Thomas said to him, "My Lord and my God!"

Thomas had kept on doubting for the full seven days, but after seeing the resurrected Jesus, the change in him was complete and immediate. As we see in verse 28. He needs no more proof that Jesus is indeed risen, or that he is the Son Of God. Thomas spent the rest of his life teaching about Jesus and his crucifixion and resurrection from the dead, and tradition has it he was killed with a sword for teaching these things.

I wonder why there were seven days between these two appearances, and why Thomas was not present the first time Jesus appeared to his disciples. Maybe it was for us to see the determination of Thomas sticking to his guns for seven days and refusing to be persuaded, but demanding physical proof of Christ's return from the dead. Then his total acceptance after he saw the resurrected Jesus. His story is powerful proof that our Lord is indeed alive today.

As an extra encouraging note to future Christians, and that is us, Jesus says in the next verse. Those who have not seen Him but still believe are blessed. Read verse 29 to see this very reassuring message from our Lord.

Joh 20:29 Then Jesus told him, "Because you have seen me, you have believed; blessed are those who have not seen and yet have believed."

It is my thoughts that God made certain that Thomas was not present a week earlier because he knew the heart and mind of Thomas and that he would stubbornly continue to say "I will not believe" until he had the absolute proof he needed.

If Jesus had not returned and shown Himself to Thomas, then our good friend Thomas, no longer Doubting Thomas, would have never believed, but this stubborn man was now convinced, and we can also believe that Jesus was resurrected thanks to the change in Thomas's attitude after he saw Jesus resurrected.

James The Brother Of Jesus

James, the half-brother of Jesus, is another perfect example of someone who has seen Jesus rise from the dead. He and the other half-brothers of Jesus did not believe that he was who he claimed to be while he was alive, and we can read this in John chapter seven and verses one through five.

Joh 7:1 After these things, Jesus was walking in Galilee, for he wouldn't walk in Judea, because the Jews sought to kill him.

Joh 7:2 Now the feast of the Jews, the Feast of Booths, was at hand.

Joh 7:3 His brothers therefore said to him, "Depart from here, and go into Judea, that your disciples also may see your works which you do.

Joh 7:4 For no one does anything in secret, and himself seeks to be known openly. If you do these things, reveal yourself to the world.

Joh 7:5 For even his brothers didn't believe in him.

We read in verse five that his half-brothers did not believe that he was "The Christ". Yet, in verse three, they tell Jesus to go to Judea so his disciples can see the works that he does. Therefore, they must have seen, or at least heard, about some miracles Jesus had performed. But they still did not believe. The following verses are more proof of this in Matthew chapter thirteen and verses fifty-four to fifty-eight.

Mat 13:54 Coming into his own country, he taught them in their synagogue, so that they were astonished, and said, "Where did this man get this wisdom, and these mighty works?

Mat 13:55 Isn't this the carpenter's son? Isn't his mother called Mary, and his brothers, James, Joses, Simon, and Judas?

Mat 13:56 Aren't all of his sisters with us? Where then did this man get all of these things?"

Mat 13:57 They were offended by him. But Jesus said to them, "A prophet is not without honor, except in his own country, and in his own house."

Mat 13:58 He didn't do many mighty works there because of their unbelief.

This is an interesting passage of scripture for anyone who still believes that Mary, the mother of Jesus, remained a virgin all her life. It is very clear here that Jesus was in his hometown, so the people gathered there would have known Jesus and his family very well. The fact Jesus had siblings was recorded here to let us know, from God's bible that Mary was only a virgin till the day Jesus was born. If you doubt this, then read Mat 1:23-25.

Mat 1:23 "Behold, the virgin shall be with child, and shall give birth to a son. They shall call his name Immanuel;" which is, being interpreted, "God with us."

Mat 1:24 Joseph arose from his sleep, and did as the angel of the Lord commanded him, and took his wife to himself;

Mat 1:25 and didn't know her sexually until she had given birth to her firstborn son. He named him Jesus.

How clear does God need to make this before people will believe the truth and accept what he has written in his precious book for our benefit? Note especially verse fifty-seven, where Jesus states a Prophet is not without honour EXCEPT in his own town and in his own home. We know from the story of Jesus' birth that Mary and Joseph were both told by the angel what was going to happen, and exactly who their first-born son was going to be. So those of "his own home" must have been others apart from Mary and Joseph, so it can only mean the half-brothers and half-sisters of Jesus.

Yet after the resurrection of Jesus, James also became a believer and wrote the book of James in the New Testament where he describes himself as "James, a servant of God and of the Lord Jesus Christ", Why the change now, and why not believe while Jesus was alive and performing his miracles.

James, and his brothers, must have witnessed or at least heard, about the works that Jesus was performing, so why only after his death did they believe that their half Brother, Jesus, was the Lord? Very simple, they had seen him crucified and buried and had mourned for him for three days, and now they had seen the resurrected Jesus. What could be more powerful proof than to witness the power of the resurrection, to see Jesus shrug off the chains of death?

The Other Brothers Of Jesus

The other half-brothers of Jesus were also believers only after the resurrection, and we can read of this in Acts chapter one and verses thirteen to fourteen.

Act 1:13 When they had come in, they went up into the upper room, where they were staying; that is Peter, John, James, Andrew, Philip, Thomas, Bartholomew, Matthew, James the son of Alphaeus, Simon the Zealot, and Judas the son of James.

Act 1:14 All these with one accord continued steadfastly in prayer and supplication, along with the women, and Mary the mother of Jesus, and with his brothers.

Here the eleven Disciples are all named and along with them are mentioned the half-brothers of Jesus. So these half-brothers were not disciples, but half-brothers of Jesus. Many people do not believe Jesus had any siblings, but here is proof positive that he did have brothers and sisters. So, the resurrection of Jesus is the turning point for many to come to believe that he is the Son of God. Even his unbelieving half-brothers and sisters were now totally convinced.

The other disciples of Jesus were 100% convinced of who he was and were prepared to go through many hardships. To be persecuted and mistreated by many as they preached about Jesus. They witnessed the persecution and death of their Lord. Therefore, they must have known their own lives would be in danger if they continued to preach about Jesus and the coming Kingdom of God. Yet they never stopped preaching until the day they were put to death because of their faith in Jesus.

You and I can also believe that Jesus is our Lord by the witnessing of his disciples. And the incredible changes that occurred in their lives after they saw Jesus resurrected from the dead. These fishermen and a tax collector all saw the works of Jesus, saw his death and resurrection, and were the foundation members of Christ's Church.

For me, it is this amazing change in their attitudes and lives after the resurrection of Jesus Christ that seals it for me. How many of these men would have lived their lives this way? And have been prepared to suffer the kinds of death they experienced? If they knew that this was all just a fantastic lie? It makes no sense to think that any of them would do this.

Paul's Conversion

The conversion of the Apostle Paul stands as one of the most pivotal and Life-changing events in the history of Christianity. He initially persecuted early Christians, considering their beliefs as heretical to Judaism. However, his dramatic conversion on the road to Damascus not only altered the trajectory of his life, but also became a cornerstone in the spread of Christianity.

Saul, a devout Jew and a Pharisee, fervently opposed the burgeoning Christian movement. He zealously pursued and persecuted followers of Jesus, viewing them as a threat to Judaism. His pivotal moment occurred during a journey to Damascus, where he intended to arrest Christians.

What was it that changed this man so much? Simply, he saw the resurrected Jesus. In the book of Acts, we see recorded this amazing event that changed Saul, later to be renamed Paul. This was when he changed from being a true hater of Christ's disciples to being one of their most powerful allies.

Act 9:1 But Saul, still breathing threats and slaughter against the disciples of the Lord, went to the high priest,

Act 9:2 and asked for letters from him to the synagogues of Damascus, that if he found any who were of the Way, whether men or women, he might bring them bound to Jerusalem.

Act 9:3 As he travelled, he got close to Damascus, and suddenly a light from the sky shone around him.

Act 9:4 He fell on the earth, and heard a voice saying to him, "Saul, Saul, why do you persecute me?"

Act 9:5 He said, "Who are you, Lord?" The Lord said, "I am Jesus, whom you are persecuting.

Act 9:6 But rise up, and enter into the city, and you will be told what you must do."

Ananias, a disciple in Damascus, received a vision from the Lord instructing him to visit Saul. Despite initial reluctance due to Saul's reputation, Ananias obeyed. Upon laying hands on Saul, scales fell from his eyes, and he regained his sight. He was then baptized and began preaching about Jesus, astonishing those who knew his previous reputation.

Paul's conversion was profound, not merely a change in belief but a complete transformation of identity and purpose. He shifted from persecuting Christians to becoming one of the most influential figures in spreading the message of Christ.

Paul's encounter with Jesus on the road to Damascus must have been an incredible thing for Paul to experience. Paul was not a member of the original Twelve, but he was an Apostle of Jesus. He went from persecuting the church to being responsible for much of what we know today as the New Testament, and the one incident that started Paul's conversion would no doubt have been when he was confronted by the resurrected Jesus on the road to Damascus. Paul spent the rest of his life preaching about Jesus and was eventually beheaded for his beliefs. Following his conversion, Paul spent time in Arabia, then returned to Damascus as we see in Gal 1:17.

> *Gal 1:17 nor did I go up to Jerusalem to see those who were apostles before me. Instead, I went away to Arabia and then came back to Damascus.*

This is where Paul claims to have received direct revelation from Jesus Christ, shaping his understanding of the Gospel. His experiences and teachings became foundational in shaping early Christian theology and practice.

Paul's missionary journeys across the Mediterranean were instrumental in establishing Christian communities and spreading the Gospel beyond Jewish territories. His letters, comprising a significant portion of the New Testament, articulate theological concepts, ethical teachings, and guidance for the early Christian churches.

Paul had gone from persecuting the church to being a powerful witness for Jesus. When he was writing to the Corinthian Church, he explained some suffering he had undergone for Jesus. Please read his account in 2Co 11:23-28.

> *2Co 11:23 Are they servants of Christ? (I speak as one beside himself) I am more so; in labours more abundantly, in prisons more abundantly, in stripes above measure, in deaths often.*

2Co 11:24 Five times from the Jews I received forty stripes minus one.

2Co 11:25 Three times I was beaten with rods. Once I was stoned. Three times I suffered shipwreck. I have been a night and a day in the deep.

2Co 11:26 I have been in travels often, perils of rivers, perils of robbers, perils from my countrymen, perils from the Gentiles, perils in the city, perils in the wilderness, perils in the sea, perils among false brothers;

2Co 11:27 in labour and travail, in watchings often, in hunger and thirst, in fastings often, and in cold and nakedness.

2Co 11:28 Besides those things that are outside, there is that which presses on me daily: anxiety for all the assemblies.

These are some hardships that Paul had to face, yet he never flinched or wavered from speaking the truth about Jesus. He would never have done this if he knew Jesus was a fake and not the Messiah, if he knew Jesus was not the real deal, then why would he continue to preach about him and be prepared to suffer so much punishment, his body bore many scars from the 195 lashes that he received, not to mention the other injuries he suffered. Why would he be prepared to suffer all this if Jesus was a phony?

We must remember where Paul came from. He had a very comfortable lifestyle until he met Jesus. We can see this in Philippians chapter three and verses three to six.

Php 3:3 For we are the circumcision, who worship God in the Spirit, and rejoice in Christ Jesus, and have no confidence in the flesh;

Php 3:4 though I myself might have confidence even in the flesh. If any other man thinks that he has confidence in the flesh, I yet more:

Php 3:5 circumcised the eighth day, of the stock of Israel, of the tribe of Benjamin, a Hebrew of Hebrews; concerning the law, a Pharisee;

Php 3:6 concerning zeal, persecuting the assembly; concerning the righteousness which is in the law, found blameless.

Paul was highly regarded among his fellow Jews before his conversion on the road to Damascus. They would have looked up to him with respect and admiration. He probably had the best seats at festivals and Jewish feasts. His opinions on all matters would have been sought after. He was a man of importance and held in high regard by the Pharisees and Sadducees of his day. But all this ended on the road to Damascus.

The question we must ask here is, why would he give this way of life up and then be hated by the Jews and punished for his ideas? Unless, of course, he knew Jesus was the real deal. And then in the next five verses, we see what the past lifestyle of Paul now meant for him.

Php 3:7 However, I consider those things that were gain to me as a loss for Christ.

Php 3:8 Yes most certainly, and I count all things to be a loss for the excellency of the knowledge of Christ Jesus, my Lord, for whom I suffered the loss of all things, and count them nothing but refuse, that I may gain Christ

Php 3:9 and be found in him, not having a righteousness of my own, that which is of the law, but that which is

through faith in Christ, the righteousness which is from God by faith;

Php 3:10 that I may know him, and the power of his resurrection, and the fellowship of his sufferings, becoming

conformed to his death;

Php 3:11 if by any means I may attain to the resurrection from the dead.

In verse eight, the term refuse, or garbage is used, but other versions of the bible are a little more graphic and say dung. So I think this gives us a rather powerful sign of what Paul thought of his former way of life and all the trapping of comfort and privileges that he once enjoyed. But now that he has found Jesus, he sees all this comfort and privilege to be worth nothing.

Paul was a changed man after seeing his risen Lord. The other disciples would no doubt have had a similar view of their former lifestyles. They did not have the same position in life as that of Paul, but they gave up their former ways of life to follow Jesus and to suffer for his name's sake. We can only imagine what they suffered as they preached about the Kingdom of God.

The significance of Paul's conversion extends beyond his personal transformation. It symbolizes the inclusivity of the Christian message – that even one vehemently opposed to the faith could undergo a radical change and become its ardent proponent. His conversion narrative illustrates the life-changing power of encountering Christ, emphasizing the universality of grace and redemption.

Moreover, Paul's conversion highlights the idea of divine intervention and purpose. His encounter with Jesus was not merely a chance but a deliberate act to redirect his life's course. This divine intervention underscores the belief that God's plans can supersede human intentions, guiding individuals toward a higher purpose.

Paul's influence on Christian theology, ethics, and practice cannot be overstated. His teachings on grace, faith, love, and the unity of believers continue to shape Christian thought and practice. His missionary efforts laid the groundwork for the global expansion of Christianity, impacting cultures and societies across centuries.

The Apostle Paul's conversion remains a source of inspiration and reflection for Christians. It signifies the potential for personal transformation, the embrace of grace, and the capacity for individuals to turn from hostility to fervent devotion. His life serves as a testament to the power of faith, perseverance, and the profound impact of encountering the divine.

In conclusion, the conversion of the Apostle Paul from a persecutor of Christians to a fervent believer and advocate for the Gospel stands as a remarkable testament to the transformative power of encountering Christ. His journey from Saul to Paul not only changed his life but also shaped the course of Christianity, leaving an indelible mark on its theology, teachings, and global expansion. Paul's conversion narrative continues to inspire believers and serves as a powerful illustration of divine grace and the potential for radical personal transformation.

How Long Was Jesus Christ in the Tomb

The question of how long Jesus was actually in the tomb is a very important topic for anyone to understand correctly. There are several differing thoughts on this matter, so it is vital to understand it from the perspective of the bible. The thoughts and teachings that originate from man cannot be relied upon to be truthful and accurate depictions of what actually happened. Therefore, as I write about this topic I will only take the evidence that we can find in the Holy Scriptures as the truth on the matter.

The greatest event to have ever happened in the entire world is undoubtedly the resurrection of our Lord and Saviour, Jesus Christ. There has always been a great deal of controversy about the crucifixion, burial, and resurrection of our Lord.

Christians have many beliefs about this all-important incident. Most Christians believe he was resurrected from the dead on the first day of the week, Sunday, and have used this belief to justify Sunday as the day they worship God. You may be surprised to learn that this is incorrect and Jesus was resurrected on the Sabbath day. Please continue to read this book to discover the truth.

With so many ideas on this topic, I will seek the truth of this topic from the only source that matters, and that is the Holy Bible. The full story from the time of Christ's crucifixion until his resurrection from the dead has been recorded in great detail in this amazing book, the holy Bible. You will need patience and be willing to search the scriptures to find the truth God has concealed in this book. The answer will not be found in just one place, a careful study of several original books of the bible will be needed to find the truth.

The Bible is the inspired word of God and must be what influences our thoughts on all things. Keep in mind the following scripture as you read this book. Also remember this verse is referring to the entire bible, not just the New Testament. Jesus quoted the bible often, and every time he quoted only from the Old Testament. This is because none of the New Testament was written while Jesus was alive on this earth. This part of the bible was written mostly by his disciples and after his crucifixion and resurrection.

2Ti 3:16 All scripture is given by inspiration of God, and is profitable for doctrine, for reproof, for correction, for instruction in righteousness:

It is my aim in this book to follow the scriptures that describe this amazing event, and find the truth that is concealed in the scriptures. If you are just seeking the truth from God's words on this very important subject, then you may be surprised at some statements I make. But please keep referring to your bible as you read this book. To come to the right conclusion, you will need to read with an open mind. If you already have an opinion on this topic, you may find it difficult to believe what I am saying. It is much harder to "unlearn" something than it is to learn a new thing. You are always influenced by your own understanding and to believe something contrary to your previously held beliefs may be difficult.

The secret to coming to the truth is always to listen to the word of God and accept what he is saying to you. You need to put man's traditions out of your mind and allow the words of the bible to convince you of the truth. Remember, if the bible tells you something different from man's teachings, then the bible is always right and should be your only source of consideration. If you accept the words of man over the words of God, then you will never learn the reality of Christ's resurrection from the dead.

I pray that our amazing God will lead you into truth from his word, The Holy Bible. Remember, this is a controversial topic, so you will need patience and time to find your answers to this issue.

How Long is Three Days and Three Nights

63

Jesus used three terms to describe how long he was to be in the tomb. Please look at these three terms. First "In three days", then "after three days", and finally "on the third day".

I believe these three terms are used to give us the precise time Jesus was in the tomb. Let us start with, "in three days". This means inside three days, it cannot be longer than three days or 72 hours. It must be equal to, or less than, exactly three days or 72 hours.

Now let us look at the term, "after three days". This means that the time can be no less than three days, it has to be equal to, but no more than 72 hours.

When you compare these 2 scriptures you can see the time Jesus was to be in the tomb had to be exactly three days, or exactly 72 hours. This is the only way it can satisfy both of these terms, "in three days", and "after three days".

Now let us look at the term "on the third day". We should always look to God's scriptures to discover how long this is, and the very best way is to go to the very first book in the bible, Genesis, and look at the first 13 verses. This describes the first three days of creation. Rather than reading all of these verses, let us look at just three.

Gen 1:5 And God called the light Day, and the darkness he called Night. And the evening and the morning were the first day.

We have had 1 period of darkness and one of light. A period of 24 hours. This is referred to as "the first day". This is followed by verse 8.

Gen 1:8 And God called the firmament Heaven. And the evening and the morning were the second day.

Now in verse 8, we have had another night and another day. Another period of 24 hours and so we have "the second day". A total of 48 hours from the start of creation. Now we come to the all-important verse 13.

Gen 1:13 And the evening and the morning were the third day.

Here the term "the third day" is used to describe the first three days of creation consisting of three nights and three days, each with 12 hours for a total of 72 hours. If you ever need a perfect description of "in three days" this is where you will find it, in the first 13 verses of the bible.

Now let us look at where these terms have been used starting with the term "in three days". It is used in the following verses to explain the time that Jesus was in the tomb.

Joh 2:13 When it was almost time for the Jewish Passover, Jesus went up to Jerusalem.

Joh 2:14 In the temple courts he found people selling cattle, sheep and doves, and others sitting at tables exchanging money.

Joh 2:15 So he made a whip out of cords, and drove all from the temple courts, both sheep and cattle; he scattered the coins of the money changers and overturned their tables.

Joh 2:16 To those who sold doves he said, "Get these out of here! Stop turning my Father's house into a market!"

Joh 2:17 His disciples remembered that it is written: "Zeal for your house will consume me."

Joh 2:18 The Jews then responded to him, "What sign can you show us to prove your authority to do all this?"

Joh 2:19 Jesus answered them, "Destroy this temple, and I will raise it again in three days."

Joh 2:20 They replied, "It has taken forty-six years to build this temple, and you are going to raise it in three days?"

Joh 2:21 But the temple he had spoken of was his body.

Joh 2:22 After he was raised from the dead, his disciples recalled what he had said. Then they believed the scripture and the words that Jesus had spoken.

In these verses, we see the Jews wanted to know who gave Jesus the authority to drive the money changers out of the temple. Jesus, knowing that they were going to crucify him, answered he would raise the temple of his body in three days. Notice that he said, "in three days". So this would mean that he was to be resurrected from the dead within three days. No longer than three days. No longer than seventy-two hours. 2 other verses that used the term "in three days" are.

> *Mar 14:58 We heard him say, I will destroy this temple that is made with hands, and within three days I will build another made without hands.*

And then in.

> *Mar 15:29 Those who passed by hurled insults at him, shaking their heads and saying, "So! You who are going to destroy the temple and build it in three days,*

Then, to empathize that he meant exactly seventy-two hours, Jesus told his disciples that "after three days" he would be raised from the tomb. Also, the Pharisees remembered Jesus had told them that after three days, he would rise again. We see this term used in the following scriptures.

> *Mar 8:31 And he began to teach them, that the Son of man must suffer many things, and be rejected of the elders, and of the chief priests, and scribes, and be killed, and after three days rise again.*

> *Mat 27:62 Now the next day, that followed the day of the preparation, the chief priests and Pharisees came together unto Pilate,*

> *Mat 27:63 Saying, Sir, we remember that that deceiver said, while he was yet alive, After three days I will rise again.*

So in these passages, we see he was to be in the tomb until "after three days". No less than three days. No less than seventy-two hours.

The last term "on the third day" is then used in these verses.

Luk 24:46 He told them, "This is what is written: The Messiah will suffer and rise from the dead on the third day,

Act 10:40 but God raised him from the dead on the third day and caused him to be seen.

1Co 15:4 that he was buried, that he was raised on the third day according to the Scriptures,

So far, we have seen three different ways to describe the time that Jesus was to be in the tomb. First was "in three days", and then "after three days", and last was "on the third day". So starting from "in three days" we can see that this is no longer than three days or seventy-two hours. Then "after three days" means that it will not be longer than three days or seventy-two hours. Then the final one is "on the third day", and we saw earlier in Genesis that the third day is after three periods of night and three periods of day, again exactly seventy-two hours.

Therefore, Jesus was in the tomb for exactly seventy-two hours. Surely, if you take scripture seriously, then how can you possibly say that Jesus was not in the tomb for **exactly seventy-two hours?** Not 71 hours, that is not long enough, and 73 hours are too long. His resurrection would have been seventy-two hours after he was laid out in the tomb. Otherwise, by his own words, he is an impostor and not the Son of God.

Therefore, with this information, we can see that the resurrection of Jesus Christ from the dead had to coincide exactly with the time Jesus was laid out in the tomb. This means that if Jesus was laid out in the tomb at 5 pm, then his resurrection from the dead had to be at precisely the same time, 5 pm three days and three nights later.

Many people want to use the measuring of three days and three nights by using other than biblical methods of measuring time or using man's traditions. I am more than happy to go with the word of God on this and say that three days and three nights are equal to exactly seventy-two hours. Some will claim that any part of a day will count as 1 day. Therefore, if you count days from five minutes before the end of a day, that five minutes counts as one day. If you use this method of calculating the time that Jesus was in the tomb, then it can vary from about forty-nine hours to seventy-two hours. This certainly is not biblical, as we saw from the Genesis 1:13 account of the term "The third day".

This is where you must decide if you will believe the written word of God, the Bible. Or are you going to accept the words and the traditions of man? This will possibly be one of the most important decisions you will make in your life. This is where we must remember what Jesus told his accusers in.

Mat 12:39 He answered, "A wicked and adulterous generation asks for a sign! But none will be given it except the sign of the prophet Jonah.

Here it states that the only sign that he will give them is the sign of Jonah, that he will be three days and three nights in the heart of the earth. It is not possible to squeeze this time frame into a Good Friday crucifixion and a Sunday morning resurrection. At the most, you will get one part day, Friday, and one full day, Saturday, and only two nights, Friday and Saturday. Certainly not the required amount of time to prove that Jesus is the Messiah. Earlier I said if he was not in the tomb for the time he predicted, then he is an impostor and not the Son of God as he claims to be.

Now we do know the time of the day that Jesus was laid in the tomb. This is recorded in Luk 23:52-54.

Luk 23:52 Going to Pilate, he asked for Jesus' body.

Luk 23:53 Then he took it down, wrapped it in linen cloth and placed it in a tomb cut in the rock, one in which no one had yet been laid.

Luk 23:54 It was Preparation Day, and the Sabbath was about to begin.

Verse 54 states that the Sabbath was drawing near, Therefore it must have been just before sunset that Jesus was laid in the tomb. We have already established the fact that Jesus had to be in the tomb for exactly 72 hours to fulfil the prophecy of the "sign of Jonah". This can only mean that Jesus was resurrected from the dead exactly 72 hours later, or just before sunset three days and three nights after he was placed in the tomb.

In the chapter titled "on what day was Jesus crucified" I will determine the day of our Lord's death and burial. Then from there, we can easily deduce the exact day, and the time of the day that Jesus Christ was resurrected from the dead.

When Paul wrote his first letter to the Corinthians, he gave us some important information that we must also consider. And this is that Jesus was crucified, buried, and resurrected "according to the scriptures" as we see in 1Co 15:1-4.

> *1Co 15:1 Now, brothers and sisters, I want to remind you of the gospel I preached to you, which you received and on which you have taken your stand.*

> *1Co 15:2 By this gospel you are saved, if you hold firmly to the word I preached to you. Otherwise, you have believed in vain.*

> *1Co 15:3 For what I received I passed on to you as of first importance: that Christ died for our sins according to the Scriptures,*

> *1Co 15:4 that he was buried, that he was raised on the third day according to the Scriptures,*

To come to any other conclusion is to ignore what the Bible has plainly told us, and to believe in a man-made theory that is definitely not Biblical. Again, I will say that I take my evidence from what the Bible shows. Anything different will not stand the test of scripture.

The Sign of Jonah

Let us start the search for the truth when some of the Pharisees asked Jesus for a sign that He was their Messiah. Jesus answered them, as we see in Matthew 12:38-40.

Mat 12:38 Then some of the Pharisees and teachers of the law said to him, "Teacher, we want to see a sign from you."

Mat 12:39 He answered, "A wicked and adulterous generation asks for a sign! But none will be given it except the sign of the prophet Jonah."

Mat 12:40 For as Jonah was three days and three nights in the belly of a huge fish, so the Son of Man will be three days and three nights in the heart of the earth.

The Pharisees and the teachers of the law did not recognise Jesus as their Messiah. Even though they understood the scriptures very well, they knew their Messiah was due at about this time. So they were looking for their Messiah to come, but they did not recognise Jesus as being their Lord. That is why they ask Jesus in verse 38 for a sign, or a miracle, that he was who he claimed to be.

Notice in verse 39, that Jesus tells them He would give them only one sign. Even though he had already performed many miracles, they wanted a powerful sign to prove who he was. Something that would prove conclusively that he was the Messiah. So, as we see in verse 39, Jesus gave them the only sign that would satisfy their demand for absolute proof. He gave them the sign of the Prophet Jonah. Jesus tells them He would be three days and three nights in the heart of the earth, or the tomb. Since this is the only sign, then it is vital He was actually in the tomb for that period of time.

There is a vital clue to the whole question about the burial and resurrection of Jesus. But we must understand exactly what Jesus meant when he said the only sign he would give them was the sign of Jonah, as recorded in Luke 11:29.

Luk 11:29 As the crowds increased, Jesus said, "This is a wicked generation. It asks for a sign, but none will be given it except the sign of Jonah.

The Pharisees asked Jesus for a sign to show that He is the promised Messiah, and the answer Jesus gave them is absolutely vital for us to understand correctly. Jesus said that the ONLY SIGN that he would give them is that He would be **three days and three nights in the heart of the earth.** The same time Jonah was in the belly of the huge fish.

Please notice that this is the ONLY SIGN that He was going to give them. Therefore, if He was not in the heart of the earth for that exact amount of time, then He is not who He claims to be, the Son Of God. If He is there for either a longer or a shorter period, then He is an impostor, a fraud, and not the Son Of God. But if he fulfilled this sign, then he is who he claims to be. Our Lord and our God.

In the book of Jonah, we can see the reference to this term Jesus used as His only sign that He is the Messiah in Jon 1:17.

Jonah 1:17 Now the LORD provided a huge fish to swallow Jonah, and Jonah was in the belly of the fish three days and three nights.

This is the sign of Jonah. Three days and three nights in the fish's belly. In Luke 11:29 and Matt 12:39, we see Jesus saying that He would give only one sign He was the Messiah, and that was the "sign of Jonah".

Surely there is enough proof in these verses to show that Jesus was in the tomb for exactly three days and three nights. And in the example from Genesis in the next chapter, we can clearly see that it cannot be anything less than a full 72 hours.

What is a Preparation Day

Hopefully, by now we can see that Jesus was exactly three days and three nights in the tomb. If you still refuse to accept this, then I suggest you listen again to the evidence I have provided and listen carefully to the scriptures quoted. The evidence I have provided for the time Jesus was in the tomb is **according to scripture.**

Now I will endeavor to show on what days, and what time of the day Jesus was buried and resurrected.

Two very important days occurred at the time of Jesus' crucifixion. The meaning of these days is vital to understand. But remember, these days are Jewish days. So the only way to understand their meaning is to look into the scriptures describing this event. Again, you will need to search the scriptures for the answer, but it is there. These two days that occurred at the time Jesus was crucified were "preparation day" and "Special Sabbath". It is very important to understand the meaning of these days, and when they occur concerning the timing of the crucifixion and resurrection of Jesus.

Preparation day, as observed in Judaism, is the day immediately before any Sabbath day. To enforce their strict observance of the Sabbath day, the Sadducees and Pharisees were to make preparations for the Sabbath well before the actual starting time of the Sabbath. All meals were to be prepared before sunset, so the only thing to do on the Sabbath day was to serve the food. This practice was to make certain that no work of any kind was done on the Sabbath. Therefore, the day before any Sabbath is called a preparation day.

Another tradition the Jews kept was to not have any bodies left hanging on the cross during the Sabbath. Therefore, they approached Pilate to have the body of Jesus, and the two thieves that were crucified with Him taken down and buried before sunset. This is made clear in Mar 15:42-43.

Mar 15:42 It was Preparation Day (that is, the day before the Sabbath). So as evening approached,

Mar 15:43 Joseph of Arimathea, a prominent member of the Council, who was himself waiting for the kingdom of God, went boldly to Pilate and asked for Jesus' body.

Here in verse 42, it is clarified that the day Jesus was crucified was on the "preparation day". This was followed by a Sabbath day, and from Joh 19:31 below it was not an ordinary Sabbath. But it was a "Special Sabbath". After Jesus died on the cross, the Jews asked Pilate for the bodies that they may be buried before the Sabbath day began, as we see in Joh 19:30-31.

Joh 19:30 When he had received the drink, Jesus said, "It is finished." With that, he bowed his head and gave up his spirit.

Joh 19:31 Now it was the day of Preparation, and the next day was to be a special Sabbath. Because the Jewish leaders did not want the bodies left on the crosses during the Sabbath, they asked Pilate to have the legs broken and the bodies taken down.

Notice it was on "the preparation day" that the Jews asked for the bodies. The following day was not just an ordinary Sabbath. It was a "Special Sabbath". The weekly Sabbath is never referred to as a "Special Sabbath". This term is reserved for special holy days throughout the year. In the next chapter, I will further explain what a "Special Sabbath" is and when they occur.

The title 'Preparation Day' is referred to 6 times in the New Testament, and each time it is mentioned, it is the day that Jesus was crucified. This day was followed by a **special Sabbath.**

Joh 19:31 Now it was the day of Preparation, and the next day was to be a special Sabbath. Because the Jewish leaders did not want the bodies left on the crosses during the Sabbath, they asked Pilate to have the legs broken and the bodies taken down.

Jesus was crucified and buried on this "preparation day". We can see this from Joh 19:31. It was on this day that the chief priests went to Pilate and requested the bodies be taken down from the crosses so they could be buried before the "Special Sabbath" began.

Without a proper understanding of these scriptures, many people will assume the term "Special Sabbath" refers to the normal weekly Sabbath. And that the preparation day was on a Friday, but this is not correct. I will elaborate more on this in the next chapter.

The most important thing I hope you will understand from this chapter is that the Sabbath following the burial of Jesus was a "Special Sabbath",

Those who believe in the Good Friday Crucifixion of Jesus, accept the day of preparation mentioned in the above verses, which refers to the preparation day that occurs just before a weekly Saturday Sabbath. But notice that in the book of John 19:31, where this Sabbath is called **a special Sabbath.**

Jesus Christ died the day before a special Sabbath, and he was put into the tomb just before the day of preparation ended. Just before the special Sabbath was about to start. Now let me prove to you that this is not the usual Saturday Sabbath, but is the day before the Passover. This is evident from John 19:14-15.

> *Joh 19:14 It was the day of Preparation of the Passover; it was about noon. "Here is your king," Pilate said to the Jews.*

> *Joh 19:15 But they shouted, "Take him away! Take him away! Crucify him!" "Shall I crucify your king?" Pilate asked. "We have no king but Caesar," the chief priests answered.*

One very important passage here is in verse 14. We see that the day Jesus was crucified was on **the preparation day for the Passover**, and not for the weekly Sabbath. This is where many people mistake this preparation day as being just before a weekly Sabbath, but it is just before the Passover Sabbath on the fifteenth day of the first month. Please read carefully the following explanation of what a "Special Sabbath" is.

What is a Special Sabbath

People in the Western world do not follow the practices of the Jews when it comes to the time when days start and finish. We have also abandoned the holy days of the bible for the new Christian seasons like Advent, Lent, Christmas, and Easter. Our days begin and end at midnight instead of the biblical time of sunset.

We need to understand the Hebrew calendar to fully understand the activities of Jesus during his earthly ministry and especially how the holy days relate to his crucifixion, death, and burial.

The first month on the Hebrew calendar is Nisan. On the 14th day is Passover and the 15th day is the first day of unleavened bread as we can see in Num 28:16-18.

Num 28:16 And in the fourteenth day of the first month is the passover of the LORD.

Num 28:17 And in the fifteenth day of this month is the feast: seven days shall unleavened bread be eaten.

Num 28:18 In the first day shall be an holy convocation; ye shall do no manner of servile work therein:

The 15th is a high day Sabbath because it is the first day of the feast of unleavened bread. The last day of this feast is also a holy day recorded in verse 25.

Num 28:25 And on the seventh day ye shall have an holy convocation; ye shall do no servile work.

There are seven high days, or "Special Sabbaths" throughout the year that are observed by Jews and a minority of Christians. These days can fall on any day of the week, as they are set on special dates in each month.

The "Special Sabbaths" are on appointed dates in a month and therefore do not fall on a weekly Sabbath. The Passover is always during the first month of the year according to the Jewish calendar, as we can see from Num 28:16-18 above.

These 2 high day Sabbaths during the feast of unleavened bread are the first 2 high day Sabbaths for the year, the other 5 "Special Sabbaths" are Pentecost, Trumpets, Atonement, and two during the Feast of Tabernacles.

The weekly Sabbath is never referred to as a high day unless a high day happens to fall on the weekly Sabbath. This can happen because these days are on monthly days and not weekdays.

From this information, we can see that Passover which is not a high day Sabbath is followed by the first day of unleavened bread that is a high day. Therefore Jesus was put into the tomb on Passover just before this high day Sabbath began.

On What Day Was Jesus Crucified

The best and most accurate way to find the day and time of Christ's burial and resurrection is to follow the activities of the women between the time of his death and burial, until the time of his resurrection. They hold the answer to the question of when Jesus was buried and resurrected from the grave.

One point I found very interesting about this, is that the women hold all of the clues that will lead us to the correct conclusion on this matter. Yet in the days of Jesus Christ, women were thought of as lower-class citizens and their testimonies held very little value in a court. This is much the same today in many countries around the world.

I believe God reveals the truth to us through the activities of the women. Follow their responses to what happened on that fateful day. Observe their obedience to the Sabbath commandments for both the weekly Sabbath, and the Sabbath marking the start of the feast of unleavened bread.

These remarkable women were used by God to show us that He does not regard our women as lower-class citizens, but sees us all as equals. Jesus had many women following him during his ministry, and most of them supported him financially, as some of them were wealthy women in their own right. Jesus never looked at women as being inferior but rather saw all of his followers as brothers and sisters.

I believe God used the activities of the women from the time Jesus was crucified until he rose from the grave to reveal when these events happened. Maybe this is God's way of telling us we are all equal in his eyes.

This most important day in all of our history has many different parts to it, and the women hold the key to unlocking the truth about the day, and the time, Jesus was crucified, buried, and resurrected from the dead. Follow their story for yourself, and uncover the lies many believe about our Lord's final hours and his resurrection from the dead.

Let us start with the narrative from Luk 23:46-56 and see that the women were all there when Jesus was crucified and put into the tomb.

Luk 23:46 And when Jesus had cried with a loud voice, he said, Father, into thy hands I commend my spirit: and having said thus, he gave up the ghost.

Luk 23:47 Now when the centurion saw what was done, he glorified God, saying, Certainly this was a righteous man.

Luk 23:48 And all the people that came together to that sight, beholding the things which were done, smote their breasts, and returned.

Luk 23:49 And all his acquaintance, and the women that followed him from Galilee, stood afar off, beholding these things.

Luk 23:50 And, behold, there was a man named Joseph, a counsellor; and he was a good man, and a just:

Luk 23:51 (The same had not consented to the counsel and deed of them;) he was of Arimathaea, a city of the Jews: who also himself waited for the kingdom of God.

Luk 23:52 This man went unto Pilate, and begged the body of Jesus.

Luk 23:53 And he took it down, and wrapped it in linen, and laid it in a sepulchre that was hewn in stone, wherein never man before was laid.

Luk 23:54 And that day was the preparation, and the sabbath drew on.

Luk 23:55 And the women also, which came with him from Galilee, followed after, and beheld the sepulchre, and how his body was laid.

Luk 23:56 And they returned, and prepared spices and ointments; and rested the sabbath day according to the commandment.

In verse forty-nine, the women who had followed Jesus were all there, standing at a distance. Verse fifty-five tells us the women saw the tomb and how his body was laid. Therefore, they were at the tomb very late on the day Jesus was crucified, and the "Special Sabbath" was about to begin. So the women would not have had time to buy the spices necessary to anoint Jesus' body before the start of the Sabbath. Also, note that ALL the women were there, so no one could have purchased the spices before the Sabbath starting.

The women were all there witnessing the crucifixion and burial of Jesus (verse fifty-five). Then, in verse fifty-six, the women went home and prepared the spices. This sounds like they prepared the spices on that same day, the preparation day when Jesus was crucified. But if you look at Mar 16:1, it is clear they purchased the spices AFTER the "Special Sabbath".

Remember, I said at the start of this book that you will not find the answer in just one place, but that a careful study in several unique books of the bible will be needed to find the truth. Let us now look into what Mark said in chapter sixteen and verse one.

> *Mar 16:1 And when the sabbath was past, Mary Magdalene, and Mary the mother of James, and Salome, had bought sweet spices, that they might come and anoint him.*

The women would not have had time to buy these spices before the High Day Sabbath started. They were there to witness Jesus being laid out in the tomb right at sunset, and verses 54 and 55 of Luke chapter 23, shows the Sabbath was drawing near. Therefore, they would not have had time to purchase the spices before the Special Sabbath started. Purchasing and preparing the spices on the special Sabbath would have violated the Special Sabbath day law. Apart from that, any shopkeeper who would have sold these spices would have closed shop by now to prepare for the Sabbath.

A reminder of what we read in the last chapter is needed here to emphasize that this Sabbath mention here is actually a special Sabbath and not an ordinary weekly Sabbath.

> *Joh 19:30 When he had received the drink, Jesus said, "It is finished." With that, he bowed his head and gave up his spirit.*

Joh 19:31 Now it was the day of Preparation, and the next day was to be a special Sabbath. Because the Jewish leaders did not want the bodies left on the crosses during the Sabbath, they asked Pilate to have the legs broken and the bodies taken down.

Mar 16:1 informs us it was after the Special Sabbath that the women purchased the spices. So we can see that one Sabbath day has passed since Jesus was laid out in the tomb. And it is after this Sabbath the women purchased and prepared the spices.

Back to Luk 23:56, explains the women prepared the spices and then rested on the Sabbath according to the commandment before going to anoint Jesus' body. Now we have a second Sabbath in the story. After resting on the first Sabbath, the "Special Sabbath", the women purchase the spices they need and prepare them. Then they rested on the Sabbath. This one is the usual weekly Sabbath.

We know from Joh 19:31 that the Sabbath that was about to begin after Jesus was buried was "The Special Sabbath" and not the weekly Saturday Sabbath. So now, if we follow the timetable of these events, we have to come to the following conclusion.

After witnessing the burial of Jesus very late on the preparation day, too late to purchase the spices before the Special Sabbath began. The women rested on the Special Sabbath. Then they purchased and prepared the spices the day after the special Sabbath. This is clear from Mar 16:1. Then, after preparing the spices, the women rested again on the weekly Sabbath, as is clear from Luk 23:56.

Luk 23:56 And they returned, and prepared spices and ointments; and rested the sabbath day according to the commandment.

From these verses, we can see two Sabbaths with one ordinary day in between. If we compare the details in both Gospels, we see where Mark tells us the women bought spices after the Sabbath (Mar 16:1). Then Luke relates they prepared the spices before resting on the weekly Sabbath (Luk 23:56). This shows two different Sabbaths being mentioned. The first, as John 19:3 tells us, was the "high day", or "Special Sabbath", which was the first day of the Feast of Unleavened Bread. The second Sabbath is the weekly Sabbath.

We saw the timetable of the events a little earlier. But now let us look at these events in reverse order to come to the exact day Jesus was crucified and buried. We know Jesus was exactly seventy-two hours in the tomb (Three days and three nights) He was put into the tomb at the very end of the day of preparation as the day was ending. Therefore, he must have risen at the same time of the day three days later.

Very early on the first day of the week, and that is Sunday, the women went to the tomb to anoint the body of Jesus. But note what was recorded in Luke chapter 24 and verses 1-3.

Luk 24:1 On the first day of the week, very early in the morning, the women took the spices they had prepared and went to the tomb.

Luk 24:2 They found the stone rolled away from the tomb,

Luk 24:3 but when they entered, they did not find the body of the Lord Jesus.

Jesus was placed in the tomb at sunset on the day he was crucified, and he had to be in the tomb for exactly seventy-two hours. This was to fulfill the prophecy he gave to the Jewish leaders that he would be in the tomb for the same time Jonah was in the whale's belly, let us recap on that section of scripture.

Mat 12:38 Then some of the Pharisees and teachers of the law said to him, "Teacher, we want to see a sign from you."

Mat 12:39 He answered, "A wicked and adulterous generation asks for a sign! But none will be given it except the sign of the prophet Jonah.

Mat 12:40 For as Jonah was three days and three nights in the belly of a huge fish, so the Son of Man will be three days and three nights in the heart of the earth.

Since he had already risen very early on the first day of the week, Sunday, he could not have risen on this day because he had to rise as the sun was setting. This only leaves the day before on the weekly Sabbath as the day for Him to be resurrected from the dead.

To determine what day Jesus was crucified, all we need to do is count backward from the time of his resurrection for exactly seventy-two hours. Starting at the end of the regular weekly Sabbath. Count back one day and this is Friday. Friday, the day after the Special Sabbath, and the day the women purchased and prepared the spices. Count back one more day and it is Thursday. This is the Special Sabbath after Jesus was crucified. This was the first day the women rested. Therefore, the day of preparation, the day of the crucifixion and burial of Jesus Christ, had to be on the Wednesday. Just before sunset.

Jesus was buried just before the sunset on the "day of preparation" on Wednesday. Therefore, he would have left the tomb just before sunset on the weekly Sabbath, exactly seventy-two hours, or three days and three nights, from the time of his burial.

This timetable fits in perfectly with the definition of "three days and three nights". Jesus told the leaders of the Jews he would be in the tomb for this exact amount of time, the same amount of time Jonah was in the belly of the enormous fish. And this was to be the <u>ONLY SIGN</u> Jesus was going to give. No other sign will conclusively prove he is our Messiah.

Even though Jesus performed many miracles, pointing to Him being God. This one sign, three days and three nights, is all he gave as the conclusive proof he was who he claimed to be. God in the flesh. The Messiah of the Jews. Our Messiah.

Also, note how the other expressions "in three days' and "after three days" fit perfectly into this timetable.

Tearing of the Curtain

The temple that stood in Jerusalem in the days Jesus Christ was on the earth was a magnificent building. According to the book of John chapter 2 verse 20, it took the Jewish people 46 years to build. When Jesus turned the tables of the money changers over in the temple courts, the Jews demanded to know by what authority Jesus had to do this. Jesus answered them as we see in John 2 verses 18-21.

Joh 2:18 The Jews therefore answered him, "What sign do you show us, seeing that you do these things?"

Joh 2:19 Jesus answered them, "Destroy this temple, and in three days I will raise it up."

Joh 2:20 The Jews therefore said, "It took forty-six years to build this temple! Will you raise it up in three days?"

Joh 2:21 But he spoke of the temple of his body.

The Jewish temple was divided into several parts, and each had a particular purpose in the worshipping of God. The innermost room was called the "Holy of Holies" and where God's presence was in the temple.

Only the High Priest could enter the "Holy of Holies", and then only once a year on the "Day Of Atonement", to atone for the sins of Israel. To enter this part of the temple at any other time of the year, or by any other person, was a sure death sentence.

This room, the holy of holies, was separated from the rest of the temple by a massive curtain or veil. The exact size of the curtain is not known, but according to Jewish tradition, the curtain was about 60 feet high. It was very thick with a thickness of about 4 inches.

So it was a massive curtain. The book of Exodus informs us how it was made. They made it from blue, purple, and scarlet materials along with twisted linen.

The veil represents the separation of a Holy God from sinful humanity because our sins have separated us from God as we see in Isa 59 verses 1 and 2.

Isa 59:1 Surely the arm of the LORD is not too short to save, nor his ear too dull to hear.

Isa 59:2 But your iniquities have separated you from your God; your sins have hidden his face from you, so that he will not hear.

As we can see from verse two, our sins have separated us from God. He designed the temple in a way to keep us separated from himself. This was the purpose of the curtain or veil.

It is well worth reading the rest of Isaiah 59 to see why the curtain was in place to make a dividing line between God (holiness) and humanity (sinfulness).

<u>The Significance.</u>

The very moment Jesus died on the cross, this massive curtain in the Temple was torn in half from the top to the bottom as recorded for us in Matthew 27 verses 50 and 51.

Mat 27:50 Jesus cried again with a loud voice, and yielded up his spirit.

Mat 27:51 Behold, the veil of the temple was torn in two from the top to the bottom. The earth quaked and the rocks were split.

The height and thickness of this veil make what happened when Jesus died on the cross even more remarkable. From verse 51, we see the curtain was torn from the top to the bottom. This would have required a massive amount of energy to tear such an enormous curtain in two. It is also interesting to note that it was torn from the top to the bottom. Signifying that it was God the Father himself who tore this massive curtain.

This was a very dramatic sign that showed us that this incredible sacrifice of Jesus was sufficient atonement for the sins of all humanity. The shedding of His blood paid for our sins and freed us from the death penalty. This opened the way into the "Holy of Holies" where the presence of God resided.

Before this amazing sacrifice of Jesus, only the high priest could enter this part of the Temple, and then only on one day of the year. What this did for us was amazing. It gave us the right to come before the "Throne of Grace" without fear. To approach Almighty God with our prayers and requests.

Now the way into the holy of holies has been opened for all people and for all time for both the Jews and the Gentiles. God also abandoned the temple and no longer lives in a dwelling made by human hands. God was now finished with the temple in Jerusalem and it was finally destroyed by the Romans in A.D. 70. We read in

> *Act 17:24 The God who made the world and all things in it, he, being Lord of heaven and earth, doesn't dwell in temples made with hands,*

The temple needed to be removed because as long as it stood, the old covenant would continue with its sacrifices. The old covenant had to make way for the new covenant to be fully established, as Hebrews 8 verse 13 shows.

> *Heb 8:13 In that he says, "A new covenant", he has made the first old. But that which is becoming old and grows aged is near to vanishing away.*

This is made even clearer in Hebrews 9 verses 8 and 9.

> *Heb 9:8 The Holy Spirit is indicating this, that the way into the Holy Place wasn't yet revealed while the first tabernacle was still standing;*

> *Heb 9:9 which is a symbol of the present age, where gifts and sacrifices are offered that are incapable, concerning the conscience, of making the worshiper perfect;*

The temple is no longer needed. We are now permitted to enter the very presence of God through this torn curtain. The writer of the book of Hebrews describes this beautifully in Hebrews 10 and verses 19 to 23.

> *Heb 10:19 Therefore, brothers and sisters, since we have confidence to enter the Most Holy Place by the blood of Jesus,*

Heb 10:20 by a new and living way opened for us through the curtain, that is, his body,

Heb 10:21 and since we have a great priest over the house of God,

Heb 10:22 let us draw near to God with a sincere heart and with the full assurance that faith brings, having our hearts sprinkled to cleanse us from a guilty conscience and having our bodies washed with pure water.

Heb 10:23 Let us hold unswervingly to the hope we profess, for he who promised is faithful.

The veil in the temple was a constant reminder to us that sin has no place in the presence of God. No amount of animal sacrifices could truly atone for the sins of mankind. But Jesus Christ, through his death on the cross, has now removed all barriers between God and man. We may now approach the throne of grace with boldness and confidence as revealed to us in Hebrews 4 and verse 16.

Heb 4:16 Let us then approach God's throne of grace with confidence, so that we may receive mercy and find grace to help us in our time of need.

We no longer need the services of a human high priest or animal sacrifices for our forgiveness. Now we have our Lord Jesus Christ in Heaven. The only one who can intercede for us with our Heavenly Father as recorded in Hebrews 7 verse 25.

Heb 7:25 Therefore he is able to save completely those who come to God through him, because he always lives to intercede for them.

The death and resurrection of our Lord Jesus Christ paid for our sins. The tearing of the curtain made it possible for all humankind to approach God. And as we can see in 1 Ti 2:5, Jesus is the only mediator between us and God.

1 Ti 2:5 For there is one God, and one mediator between God and men, the man Christ Jesus,

Many people today still rely on a priest to confess their sins to. This is no longer necessary. Understand 1 Timothy 2:5 and see there is only one mediator between God and man, and that is Jesus Christ. No one else can intercede for us. No one else, no saint, no angel, no man, and definitely no woman has the authority to intercede between God and mankind. This prerogative has been reserved for Jesus Christ and him alone.

The Thief on The Cross Alongside Jesus

What can we learn from the thief who was crucified on the cross alongside Jesus? Why was this incident recorded at all, and can we learn anything important from this event?

First, let us consider who this person was. There is nowhere in recorded history for us to determine what the lifestyle was of this thief. But we can presume he was not an amiable person. He was a thief, and who knows what other crimes he may have committed to earn the death sentence? In the book of Luke, we see the confession of this criminal. He admits he is guilty and deserving of the penalty he is now about to pay.

It is very important to note here that he also says Jesus has done nothing wrong. Then he calls Jesus Lord and then asks Jesus to remember him when He comes into His Kingdom. In doing this, he is acknowledging Jesus as his Messiah. Showing Jesus he has faith in who he is. Maybe this thief heard of some miracles Jesus had performed. Or maybe he had seen some of these miracles for himself. This we do not know, but from the comments he made about Jesus, I feel he must have had some limited knowledge of who Jesus was. This event is recorded for us in Luke 23 verses 39 to 42.

> *Luk 23:39 One of the criminals who hung there hurled insults at him: "Aren't you the Messiah? Save yourself and us!"*

> *Luk 23:40 But the other criminal rebuked him. "Don't you fear God," he said, "since you are under the same sentence?*

> *Luk 23:41 We are punished justly, for we are getting what our deeds deserve. But this man has done nothing wrong."*

> *Luk 23:42 Then he said, "Jesus, remember me when you come into your kingdom."*

When we consider this event, we realise the following points about this criminal. He would not have been baptised. Nor had he ever followed Jesus nor prayed to Him. By his own confession, he was a thief and deserving of his penalty. He was only a matter of a few hours from his death when he asked Jesus to remember him.

A very late conversion and declaration of his belief in Jesus as "The Son Of God". This fits in very well with what we hear in the book of Acts 2:21.

Act 2:21 And it shall come to pass, that whosoever shall call on the name of the Lord shall be saved.

This thief was calling on the name of the Lord. Therefore, he qualifies as one who can be saved. So even with his very late declaration of Jesus being the "Son of God". He is assured of a place in God's kingdom. Now read the amazing response this thief got from Jesus in Luke 23 verse 43.

Luk 23:43 Jesus answered him, "Truly I tell you, today you will be with me in paradise."

Jesus tells this thief he will be in paradise. This is the reward for the thief after his confession that Jesus is the Christ. It is also the reward millions of other people have been promised because of their faith in their Lord.

But this is also where we come upon what may be a major error in interpreting this verse. Most people will more than likely disagree with me. But if you listen to the end, I am sure you will see what I mean.

The first thing to realize is that when this was originally written in Greek, there were no punctuation marks used. Therefore, the comma used in this verse was not in the original. Those who interpreted this verse put the comma where it best suited their own beliefs and understanding. Some earlier books have the comma before the word today, while others put the comma after the word today. Consider the 2 versions of this verse below. One with the comma placed before today. Then consider the same verse with the comma after the word today, and see how it completely changes the meaning of the verse.

When the comma comes before today, as in this version. "Assuredly I tell you, today you will be with me in Paradise". This interpretation can mean the criminal will be in paradise on that very day with Jesus. But now read the same passage with the comma after the word today. As in the following version of the verse.

"Assuredly I tell you today, you will be with me in Paradise." Here Jesus tells the criminal he will be in paradise with him. but he does not say when this will happen. It will be in the future, but how long in the future Jesus does not say.

He will enter paradise when he is resurrected from the dead. The same as every other person who has died in faith.

To establish which one of these verses is correct. We must consider other passages from the Bible that concern the time when all the saved will receive their rewards and be in paradise. We must work out when each of those who have died in faith will indeed enter paradise. Will it be on the very day they die? Or will all the faithful enter the kingdom at a yet future date?

The apostle Paul teaches us that all believers who die will come forth from the graves. But only when Jesus Christ returns. This has been recorded for us in One Corinthians 15 verses 20 to 23.

1Co 15:20 But now is Christ risen from the dead, and become the firstfruits of them that slept.

1Co 15:21 For since by man came death, by man came also the resurrection of the dead.

1Co 15:22 For as in Adam all die, even so in Christ shall all be made alive.

1Co 15:23 But every man in his own order: Christ the firstfruits; afterward they that are Christ's at his coming.

We see in verse 23, that Christ is the "first fruits". He is the very first person to be made alive, or to be resurrected from the dead. This has to include all of the people from the Old Testament times who lived before the time of Jesus, otherwise, Jesus could not be the first person to be resurrected from the dead. They are all still waiting their turn to be resurrected.

The 11th chapter of Hebrews is commonly known as the "faith chapter". Here you can read the names of many of those who have lived since the world was first created. Some famous names such as Abel, Noah, Abraham the father of the faithful, and Moses. Plus others who did mighty deeds in the name of God. So now let us examine from the evidence from the bible when these mighty men and women of God received their just rewards. The proof is in the following amazing passage of scripture that describes how they lived, and how they were treated. They received promises, as we see in verse 33, but they have never received those promises, as we see in verse 39. Please listen to Heb 11:32-40.

Heb 11:32 And what more shall I say? I do not have time to tell about Gideon, Barak, Samson and Jephthah, about David and Samuel and the prophets,

Heb 11:33 who through faith conquered kingdoms, administered justice, and gained what was promised; who shut the mouths of lions,

Heb 11:34 quenched the fury of the flames, and escaped the edge of the sword; whose weakness was turned to strength; and who became powerful in battle and routed foreign armies.

Heb 11:35 Women received back their dead, raised to life again. There were others who were tortured, refusing to be released so that they might gain an even better resurrection.

Heb 11:36 Some faced jeers and flogging, and even chains and imprisonment.

Heb 11:37 They were put to death by stoning; they were sawed in two; they were killed by the sword. They went about in sheepskins and goatskins, destitute, persecuted and mistreated—

Heb 11:38 the world was not worthy of them. They wandered in deserts and mountains, living in caves and in holes in the ground.

Heb 11:39 These were all commended for their faith, yet none of them received what had been promised,

Heb 11:40 since God had planned something better for us so that only together with us would they be made perfect.

Verse 35 here tells of women receiving their dead raised to life, This is a very temporary raising to life, they were not given eternal life, otherwise, they would still be here with us today. How long they lived we do not know but they died again and returned to their graves.

These amazing people who served God before Jesus came to the earth, are yet to receive their rewards, as we can see in verse 39. Then in verse 40, they will not be made perfect without the apostles. They will not enter God's kingdom apart from, or before, the apostles of Jesus Christ.

In all of Paul's writing, there is nowhere he ever tries to comfort the living, by telling them that their deceased loved ones are already with Jesus in heaven. He always attempts to bring peace into their hearts by reminding them of the resurrection of the dead.

This I will show you in the following sections of scripture. First, in the book of John, then in 1 Thessalonians, and then again back in the book of John. Listen to what we are told in John 5:28-29.

> *Joh 5:28 "Do not be amazed at this, for a time is coming when all who are in their graves will hear his voice*

> *Joh 5:29 and come out—those who have done what is good will rise to live, and those who have done what is evil will rise to be condemned.*

Notice in these verses that all those in their tombs, or their graves, will hear his voice and come out of their graves and be resurrected. All those mean everyone who has ever lived and died. Some resurrected to eternal life, and some to judgment.

When Lazarus, the brother of Martha, died, Martha was aware of the fact that Lazarus would be resurrected from the dead on "the last day". This is clear from her conversation with Jesus just before he went to the tomb of Lazarus and raised him from the dead. Recorded in Joh 11:23-25.

> *Joh 11:23 Jesus said to her, "Your brother will rise again."*

> *Joh 11:24 Martha answered, "I know he will rise again in the resurrection at the last day."*

Joh 11:25 Jesus said to her, "I am the resurrection and the life. The one who believes in me will live, even though they die;

Lazarus, a wonderful friend of Jesus, will be raised from the dead on "the last day" when Jesus Christ returns in all power and glory. This we saw in the book of John above when all who are in their graves will come out. Now let us look at when this resurrection is going to take place. Listen to 1Th 4:15-18.

1Th 4:15 According to the Lord's word, we tell you that we who are still alive, who are left until the coming of the Lord, will certainly not precede those who have fallen asleep.

1Th 4:16 For the Lord himself will come down from heaven, with a loud command, with the voice of the archangel and with the trumpet call of God, and the dead in Christ will rise first.

1Th 4:17 After that, we who are still alive and are left will be caught up together with them in the clouds to meet the Lord in the air. And so we will be with the Lord forever.

1Th 4:18 Therefore encourage one another with these words.

Here in verse 16, we can see when this resurrection of the dead will take place. It will be when Jesus returns from Heaven and not before.

Paul again talks about the resurrection of the dead, and not only his hope for the resurrection but also the hope of the Pharisees of his day. They also believed there would be a resurrection of the dead, both for the just and the unjust. Paul confesses his faith in the resurrection of the dead in Acts 24 verses 14 and 15.

Act 24:14 However, I admit that I worship the God of our ancestors as a follower of the Way, which they call a sect. I believe everything that is in accordance with the Law and that is written in the Prophets,

Act 24:15 and I have the same hope in God as these men themselves have, that there will be a resurrection of both the righteous and the wicked.

In these scriptures, we see the dead will be rewarded and resurrected from the dead at the resurrection of the righteous. This will happen only when Jesus returns, not before.

Now let us return to the story of the thief on the cross. How can it be claimed the criminal crucified with Jesus went into paradise, or was resurrected, the day he died on the cross? If this is the case, then he would be the only one to have ever died, and gone straight to Heaven that very same day.

There is one vital piece of evidence we are yet to look at. The day Jesus died, he was placed in the tomb where he remained for three days and three nights. Then, at the end of this time, he was met by Mary when she was looking for his body. We read about this encounter in John 20 verses 16 and 17.

Joh 20:16 Jesus said to her, "Mary." She turned toward him and cried out in Aramaic, "Rabboni!" (which means "Teacher").

Joh 20:17 Jesus said, "Do not hold on to me, for I have not yet ascended to the Father. Go instead to my brothers and tell them, 'I am ascending to my Father and your Father, to my God and your God.'"

It is very important to understand what Jesus said the Mary in these verses. Remember he has been in the tomb for three days and three nights since the day he died on the cross. He said to her. "Don't hold me, **for I haven't yet ascended to my father**". Do you understand what this means? Three days and three nights after he died on the cross he still has not ascended to Heaven. Then he tells Mary. "I am ascending to my Father and your Father". Now he tells Mary, he is about to go to his Father in Heaven, Therefore, if he has not yet ascended to his Father before meeting Mary at the tomb, then he did not ascend on the day he was crucified. If Jesus did not ascend on the day he was crucified, then the thief also could not have ascended on that day.

Let us look again at

Luk 23:43 Jesus answered him, "Truly I tell you, today you will be with me in paradise."

If, as in the example above, the coma comes before the word today, then Jesus and the thief went to Heaven on the day they were crucified. But as we have just witnessed, Jesus did not ascend to his Father for another 72 hours. Therefore, the thief could not have possibly gone to Heaven on the day he was crucified either. The only plausible explanation is that the coma was in the incorrect place in Luk 23:43. When the coma comes after the word today it all makes perfect sense. Jesus told the thief he would one day be in paradise, at the same time all other believers in Jesus would enter paradise.

This thief who had done nothing to deserve God's grace, except to call upon the name of Jesus, is now assured by Jesus he will enter paradise. This will be with the rest of the resurrected dead at the return of Jesus Christ at the very end of this age. The example of this thief in the Bible is to make very clear to us the meaning of John 3:16. Whoever believes in Him, and it does not matter how late they believe, all that matters is that they believe. They will be in paradise.

One aspect of this is to realise that it does not matter how late in your life you believe in Jesus Christ you are guaranteed a place in his kingdom. If you doubt this fact, then read the parable of the workers in the vineyard recorder in Mat 20:1-16.

Mat 20:1 "For the kingdom of heaven is like a landowner who went out early in the morning to hire workers for his vineyard.

Mat 20:2 He agreed to pay them a denarius for the day and sent them into his vineyard.

Mat 20:3 "About nine in the morning he went out and saw others standing in the marketplace doing nothing.

Mat 20:4 He told them, 'You also go and work in my vineyard, and I will pay you whatever is right.'

Mat 20:5 So they went. "He went out again about noon and about three in the afternoon and did the same thing.

Mat 20:6 About five in the afternoon he went out and found still others standing around. He asked them, 'Why have you been standing here all day long doing nothing?'

Mat 20:7 "'Because no one has hired us,' they answered. "He said to them, 'You also go and work in my vineyard.'

Mat 20:8 "When evening came, the owner of the vineyard said to his foreman, 'Call the workers and pay them their wages, beginning with the last ones hired and going on to the first.'

Mat 20:9 "The workers who were hired about five in the afternoon came and each received a denarius.

Mat 20:10 So when those came who were hired first, they expected to receive more. But each one of them also received a denarius.

Mat 20:11 When they received it, they began to grumble against the landowner.

Mat 20:12 'These who were hired last worked only one hour,' they said, 'and you have made them equal to us who have borne the burden of the work and the heat of the day.'

Mat 20:13 "But he answered one of them, 'I am not being unfair to you, friend. Didn't you agree to work for a denarius?

Mat 20:14 Take your pay and go. I want to give the one who was hired last the same as I gave you.

Mat 20:15 Don't I have the right to do what I want with my own money? Or are you envious because I am generous?'

Mat 20:16 "So the last will be first, and the first will be last."

In this parable, we see the householder in verse one, paid the workers who only worked for the last hour of the day the same amount as those who worked the entire day. Their rewards are the same. This principle is the same with those who come to accept Jesus Christ as their lord and saviour very late in their lives. God wants to treat us all the same and give us all the same reward, eternal life in his kingdom. And as we saw in the example of the thief on the cross, he was promised entry into paradise when he had but a few very short hours to live. All believers get the same reward. Entry into paradise.

Faith in "The Son Of God" is all that matters to be saved. No good work will ever get you there. Only faith in Jesus Christ as your Lord and saviour will save you. But just like the criminal on the cross, you will not receive your reward until Jesus Christ returns and resurrects all people from all times. Some to eternal life and some to the judgment.

Why is the resurrection so important

The resurrection of Jesus Christ from the tomb is the most important belief for any Christian to hold and believe. To acknowledge the death of Jesus on the cross and all that means for Christians is important. This is because, by his death, he died for the forgiveness of our sins. Without this amazing self-sacrifice, we would all still be in our sins.

Christ's dying on the cross is one thing, but his resurrection from the dead is the centre of redemption for everyone. If there is not an empty tomb, then there is no resurrection. And if there is no resurrection from the dead of Jesus Christ, then he is not who he claims to be. The Son of God, our Messiah. Without the resurrection, what Jesus came to do must end in defeat and disillusion for us all.

It is only from the words we see in Mat 28:1-7 that we can have confidence in Jesus Christ having the power over death and Satan.

Mat 28:1 After the Sabbath, at dawn on the first day of the week, Mary Magdalene and the other Mary went to look at the tomb.

Mat 28:2 There was a violent earthquake, for an angel of the Lord came down from heaven and, going to the tomb, rolled back the stone and sat on it.

Mat 28:3 His appearance was like lightning, and his clothes were white as snow.

Mat 28:4 The guards were so afraid of him that they shook and became like dead men.

Mat 28:5 The angel said to the women, "Do not be afraid, for I know that you are looking for Jesus, who was crucified.

Mat 28:6 He is not here; he has risen, just as he said. Come and see the place where he lay.

Mat 28:7 Then go quickly and tell his disciples: 'He has risen from the dead and is going ahead of you into Galilee. There you will see him.' Now I have told you."

All four gospels end with the resurrection of Jesus from the dead. Paul, in his first letter to the Corinthians, makes it very clear how important the resurrection is. Please read the following verses and understand the meaning they contain.

1Co 15:12 But if it is preached that Christ has been raised from the dead, how can some of you say that there is no resurrection of the dead?

1Co 15:13 If there is no resurrection of the dead, then not even Christ has been raised.

1Co 15:14 And if Christ has not been raised, our preaching is useless and so is your faith.

1Co 15:15 More than that, we are then found to be false witnesses about God, for we have testified about God that he raised Christ from the dead. But he did not raise him if in fact the dead are not raised.

1Co 15:16 For if the dead are not raised, then Christ has not been raised either.

1Co 15:17 And if Christ has not been raised, your faith is futile; you are still in your sins.

1Co 15:18 Then those also who have fallen asleep in Christ are lost.

1Co 15:19 If only for this life we have hope in Christ, we are of all people most to be pitied.

These verses describe the situation we would find ourselves in if Jesus had not told us the truth, and if Almighty God had not raised Him from the dead. The millions of people who profess to follow Him would do so in vain.

If Jesus did not rise from the tomb, then Christians have nothing to put their trust in. The bible would be irrelevant and there would be very little purpose in our lives. But since we can believe Jesus was resurrected, everything changes and our futures in God's Kingdom are certain.

If there was no resurrection

Many people do not believe in God. Therefore, they do not believe in the resurrection of Jesus Christ or any other resurrection. When they die, they just disappear and they have no future after death. A very sad thought and ending for anyone. So let us examine what the future holds for us if Jesus Christ was not resurrected from the dead. Please consider the following points.

1. Every promise Jesus has given us would be untrustworthy. Jesus promised many times he would rise from the dead. So if he failed to accomplish this, then he is to be pitied as an impostor and someone we cannot rely upon for anything. When you consider that almost the entire bible, old and New Testaments, speak of Jesus. Then his failure to beat death by not being resurrected would make the entire bible a sham.

By keeping the promise of his ability to defeat death, we can now depend completely on every other promise he has made. What could be more difficult than to beat death? So if he can do this, then every other promise would be easy for Him.

2. The resurrection is the endorsement of God the Father that Jesus Christ is the risen Lord of Lords and King of Kings. He is no longer as he was before his resurrection when he was born of a woman and lived like any other human being. Now his divine son-ship and deity are revealed and made clear.

Rom 1:4 and who through the Spirit of holiness was appointed the Son of God in power by his resurrection from the dead: Jesus Christ our Lord.

His shed blood on the cross now covers our sins and is a sure sign he will also resurrect those who believe and trust in Him. Just as he promised in the following verses from the book of John.

Joh 6:44 "No one can come to me unless the Father who sent me draws them, and I will raise them up at the last day.

Joh 6:40 For my Father's will is that everyone who looks to the Son and believes in him shall have eternal life, and I will raise them up at the last day."

Eternal life and resurrection from the dead are certain for all those who look to Jesus as the Son of God.

3. Without the resurrection, we would not have any foundation for the church. It was only the resurrection that turned the first Christians into faithful and unafraid followers of their Lord. When you compare the attitudes of Christ's disciples from before, to after his resurrection, you see a massive change in their lives. They went from being afraid and hiding from the Synagogue leaders, to boldly proclaiming the good news about Jesus.

The disciples were all killed at a relatively young age (except for John) because of their preaching. They trusted Jesus to care for them in life and death. They had witnessed Jesus defeat death and knew they would also be raised from the dead on the last day, as Jesus had promised them and us.

It is inconceivable to think these disciples would be prepared to suffer and die the way they did, if they knew Jesus was an impostor and not the real Son of God.

The gospels are all centered on the death, burial, and resurrection of Jesus Christ. But the cross does not have a lot of meaning without the all-important resurrection. Any "gospel" that does not put the cross and the resurrection together as both vital for the Christian to understand and proclaim, is not complete and not the authentic message given to us by Jesus and his disciples.

The following passage of scripture in the book of Hebrews is very reassuring. We see Jesus crowned with glory but still working to save his elect. He is the creator of all things, but he still calls us brothers and sisters.

Heb 2:9 But we do see Jesus, who was made lower than the angels for a little while, now crowned with glory and honor because he suffered death, so that by the grace of God he might taste death for everyone.

Heb 2:10 In bringing many sons and daughters to glory, it was fitting that God, for whom and through whom everything exists, should make the pioneer of their salvation perfect through what he suffered.

Heb 2:11 Both the one who makes people holy and those who are made holy are of the same family. So Jesus is not ashamed to call them brothers and sisters.

4. Without the resurrection, the millions of Christians who have been martyred would never find justice.

There would not be any final reckoning for sin. Satan, who has caused our pain and suffering in this world, would have won his struggle against God. But the resurrection of Jesus has shown us who is ultimately in control. Satan's days are numbered, and that number is growing less every day.

Jesus will return soon, even though fewer and fewer people believe this any more, and when he returns it will be in great power and not as the suffering servant from his first appearance on the earth.

Mat 16:27 For the Son of Man is going to come in his Father's glory with his angels, and then he will reward each person according to what they have done.

5. Jesus Christ led by example and taught us the principles for living a good life. In the book of Matthew, Jesus instructs us we must sacrifice our self-centered and uncaring lifestyles and consider the needs of others. He put it very clearly by saying if we lose our lives for his name's sake, we will actually find life. It sounds like an oxymoron, but it is the way to live if we want to see the resurrection become a reality in our own lives.

Mat 16:24 Then Jesus said to his disciples, "Whoever wants to be my disciple must deny themselves and take up their cross and follow me.

Mat 16:25 For whoever wants to save their life will lose it, but whoever loses their life for me will find it.

Mat 16:26 What good will it be for someone to gain the whole world, yet forfeit their soul? Or what can anyone give in exchange for their soul?

The resurrection of Jesus Christ from the dead was witnessed by many people. He has promised to return and we can be sure this will happen. It does not matter if anyone does not believe this, it will happen regardless. When this happens, he will resurrect those who are faithful to Him.

We can put our faith in the scriptures and in the understanding Jesus was resurrected from the dead, and he will do the same thing for us upon his return.

Mockers of Jesus Christ

The first thing I must do here is to define exactly what the word mocker means. One description of a mocker from the dictionary is "someone who jeers or mocks or treats something with contempt or calls out in derision". Other words that can describe a Mocker are Scoffer and Sneerer.

These mockers will actively oppose anyone who has a different perspective on life to their own beliefs. They are generally aggressive, and hostile and want nothing more than to demean those who act differently to them. They will not listen to another person's ideas but are quick to talk over their opponents.

Those we know today as "The Woke" fit this description perfectly. They, along with many governments, want nothing more than to control all people so we all have the same understanding and beliefs. They do not want anyone to have their own thoughts and beliefs. Everyone is expected to conform to their ideas.

It will be the wise followers of Jesus Christ who take his advice as we see in.

Rom 12:2 Do not conform to the pattern of this world, but be transformed by the renewing of your mind. Then you will be able to test and approve what God's will is—his good, pleasing and perfect will.

Mockers will try to draw you away from what you know is the truth. It will be difficult to resist them, but if we do not, then we will not be pleasing to God.

Mockers have been around for thousands of years. Listen to what Job from the Old Testament had to say.

Job 17:2 Surely mockers surround me; my eyes must dwell on their hostility.

Mockers have always been with us and will still be with us right up until the end when Jesus Christ returns. Listen now to what 2Ti 3:1-5 has to say.

2Ti 3:1 But mark this: There will be terrible times in the last days.

2Ti 3:2 People will be lovers of themselves, lovers of money, boastful, proud, abusive, disobedient to their parents, ungrateful, unholy,

2Ti 3:3 without love, unforgiving, slanderous, without self-control, brutal, not lovers of the good,

2Ti 3:4 treacherous, rash, conceited, lovers of pleasure rather than lovers of God—

2Ti 3:5 having a form of godliness but denying its power. Have nothing to do with such people.

Most of the traits we see recorded here fit the description of a Mocker.

Ever since the time Jesus Christ was first here on this earth. People have been waiting for his return as He promised to do. It has now been the best part of two thousand years since Jesus was crucified, resurrected from the dead, and ascended into Heaven. He made a promise to return but never told anyone how long it would be before He came back. Many Christians are now starting to ask the question. "When will He return?". While many other non-believers are saying, "He will never return".

Well, there are many signs in the world today that indicate Jesus' return is close. Closer than most people believe. One sure sign is mockers will become more prevalent. They will mock sin and make light of it, they will openly commit it and glory in it. And mostly they will scoff at religion. These are the people the Apostle Peter wrote about in his letter to the Church and recorded for us in 2Pe 3:3-4.

2Pe 3:3 Above all, you must understand that in the last days scoffers will come, scoffing and following their own evil desires.

2Pe 3:4 They will say, "Where is this 'coming' he promised? Ever since our ancestors died, everything goes on as it has since the beginning of creation."

In this modern age, we can see these mockers, or scoffers becoming more numerous and vocal. As we see from the previous verses, we must expect to encounter these people at the last times. Therefore we must not be surprised when we have to face these people, it is inevitable.

These mockers, or scorners, are becoming more evident every day as we see our world changing very fast. And most times it is not for the better. Read the following passages from the book of John to see some of the ways our world is predicted to change in these "last days". We are very close to this time in man's history. Therefore, we must be ready for what our futures hold.

Joh 15:18 "If the world hates you, keep in mind that it hated me first.

Joh 15:19 If you belonged to the world, it would love you as its own. As it is, you do not belong to the world, but I have chosen you out of the world. That is why the world hates you.

Christians must be prepared to be slandered, ridiculed, and persecuted in the years ahead. We have some sound advice from the Old Testament. Listen to what we are told.

Pro 9:7 Whoever corrects a mocker invites insults; whoever rebukes the wicked incurs abuse.

Pro 9:8 Do not rebuke mockers or they will hate you; rebuke the wise and they will love you.

You can see the difference between correcting a mocker and a wise person. The wise will listen and repent. But the mocker will just make your life as hard as he possibly can. In the book of Proverbs we have other examples of scoffers or mockers. Listen to these three examples.

Pro 13:1 A wise son heeds his father's instruction, but a mocker does not respond to rebukes.

Pro 22:10 Drive out the mocker, and out goes strife; quarrels and insults are ended.

Pro 29:8 Mockers stir up a city, but the wise turn away anger.

Now we can turn our attention to the New Testament and the book of Jude. Here we can see more evidence that mockers will be around in the last days, they will be out to satisfy their own desires and lusts. God will have no part in their lives. Listen to.

Jud 1:17 But, dear friends, remember what the apostles of our Lord Jesus Christ foretold.

Jud 1:18 They said to you, "In the last times there will be scoffers who will follow their own ungodly desires."

Jud 1:19 These are the people who divide you, who follow mere natural instincts and do not have the Spirit.

Now we understand that mockers will play a big part in the years ahead, but unfortunately, they will only be a small part of our problems. Listen to how the writer of the book of Romans describes what lies ahead for all people.

Rom 1:29 They have become filled with every kind of wickedness, evil, greed and depravity. They are full of envy, murder, strife, deceit and malice. They are gossips,

Rom 1:30 slanderers, God-haters, insolent, arrogant and boastful; they invent ways of doing evil; they disobey their parents;

Rom 1:31 they have no understanding, no fidelity, no love, no mercy.

Rom 1:32 Although they know God's righteous decree that those who do such things deserve death, they not only continue to do these very things but also approve of those who practice them.

This paints a very poor description of what our society will become. I know many people will believe that our world is too modern and sophisticated to stoop to these low levels. But over the past few decades, we have seen these characteristics becoming more prevalent, and no doubt we will see more of this type of behavior in the coming years. This world will go from bad to worse. These people will be the mockers who do not believe in Christ's return. Social media has much to answer for regarding this type of conduct in our society. And it is not reserved only for the young. Many older people also enjoy the sleazy side of social media.

Time is no barrier for God. He is outside of time because He created all things including time. God is working to His own timetable and most certainly not ours. God is not rushing into His return. He is waiting for as many people as possible to turn to Him and be saved.

Many people will say "Just show us Jesus and we will believe". Well, I am afraid that will not work. Remember what happened to Jesus when He was here the first time. The majority of people did not believe it. And even though they saw many of His miracles, it made little difference. They finally had Jesus put to death on the cross. So I doubt it would make any difference to most people today if they saw Jesus or not. They will still want to pursue their own interests. They would reject Jesus and His teachings again. They are more interested in doing their own thing.

Can you honestly imagine the paedophiles, drug barons, and those who profit from the trans-gender industry, turning to God for forgiveness? No, these people will continue to mock not only the return of Jesus but also his holy name. We can be sure of this because we have been warned by God that this is in our future. Listen to Rev 22:11.

Rev 22:11 Let the one who does wrong continue to do wrong; let the vile person continue to be vile; let the one who does right continue to do right; and let the holy person continue to be holy."

There is one thing you can rely upon, and that is God will never force anyone to accept Jesus Christ as their Lord and Saviour. He gave us all free will, but Satan has used this amazing gift from God to influence us into doing what is evil in the sight of God. This is the cause of our troubles, but God will never take away our free will. We were created in His image to have a relationship with Him. He does not need another flock of sheep. He wants us to turn to Him of our own free will.

When you see and hear people mocking the return of Jesus Christ. You can be sure it is a sign of the times. A sure sign of the return of our Lord. So do not worry when you see these mockers in the world. Just keep your eyes and mind on the return of Jesus and the promises He has made to you.

Conclusion

This book covers only a very small part of the life of our Lord Jesus Christ. I have covered a few different topics to give you an overview of Jesus, his miracles, and prophecies in the Old Testament regarding his first coming.

I believe the author of the book of 1 John sums up why I wanted to write this book. Read what he had to say in 1 John 5:13.

1Jn 5:13 I write these things to you who believe in the name of the Son of God so that you may know that you have eternal life.

About The Author

Leslie Rendell worked most of his life in an agricultural support industry, mostly in the supply of spare parts for machinery. Since his retirement in 2014 he has dedicated much of his time to bible study and writing books as he comes to understand biblical topics.

He understands the bible is a very complex book and one that is easy to misinterpret and believes this is one of the main reasons why there are so many different version of the bible and different religions around the world.

What he writes is his own interpretation of God's holy scriptures. He studies the thoughts of other writers to try to see things from their point of view, but always comes back to the bible as the final authority on any topic. His main aim in writing, is to give anyone who is seeking the truth from God's words a starting point in their own research.

Leslie's other interest are photography, and his growing family.

Don't miss out!

Visit the website below and you can sign up to receive emails whenever Leslie Rendell publishes a new book. There's no charge and no obligation.

https://books2read.com/r/B-A-VDUV-SDJBD

Connecting independent readers to independent writers.

Also by Leslie Rendell

Bible Studies
Three Days and Three Nights
According To Your Faith
Do Not Conform
How Long Was Jesus Christ in the Tomb
The Law of Moses
Abraham, Jesus and the Cross
Do We Have Immortal Souls
Be Holy
Is Being Fearful A Sin Against God
Mockers and the Return of Jesus Christ
Teachers During The Tribulation
Tearing of The Curtain in The Temple
The Thief On The Cross Alongside Jesus Christ
What Is The Rapture
The Imminence of the Rapture is a False Teaching.
Why The Pre-Tribulation Rapture Theory Is False
Are You Hindered By Satan
Satan is Targeting Man's Free Will
Why Is There So Much Suffering In Our World
The Sign of Jonah
Evil Is The Rejection Of God
Satan, Spirit Being With Many Names
Have Faith In God
Only One Sign
The Lord's Passover

The Resurrection of Jesus Christ
Jesus The Christ

Watch for more at https://www.leslierendell.com.